A HIDDEN CHILDHOOD

A HIDDEN CHILDHOOD
1942–1945

Frida Scheps Weinstein

TRANSLATED BY
Barbara Loeb Kennedy

HILL AND WANG · NEW YORK
A division of Farrar, Straus and Giroux

TO MY MOTHER

A HIDDEN CHILDHOOD

I TUG ON THE STRING a little harder. I'm afraid
the box will tear. The shoebox is jammed against the
sidewalk. It's because of my mother. She's pushing me.
We have to hurry. When I'm with my mother we're
always late. I run to free the box. My doll has come
halfway out from the jolt, and her blue eyes are almost
open. It's my first doll, which can open and close its
eyes. The scraps of cloth have come out, too. I rearrange them. I like old cloth. It's so soft when you touch
it, and you can rumple and tear it and you still have a
piece of cloth.

The passersby are laughing because the shoebox is
dragging and making a noise. They stop. They don't

see that it's a little baby carriage. My mother can't buy me a real one. I also wanted a mechanical doll that could walk by itself. My mother has no money. But we are not poor. I don't like poor people or beggars. *I* am warmly dressed and well fed. My mother says that's the main thing. She deals in the "market." Everyone says she manages very well. Aunt Ida—that's her sister—is always coming to the house to ask where she can find work. But she doesn't like to deal in the market. She loves to dress up, to play the coquette, and my mother says she is looking for a husband. Aunt Ida does everything I want. She is afraid of me. I'm a spoiled child.

We arrive at the railroad station. It's still very dark. We got up early. We can hardly see through the smoke billowing over the engine. Two cars are linked. I love it. It makes a funny noise when they touch each other where the big nails are. A very tall lady, holding two little girls by the hand, stops us on the platform. She's wearing a long black veil with a little red cross—it's the Red Cross lady. I recognize her. One of the little girls has long black stockings on. I'd like some, too.

My mother is wearing her everyday green coat. I hate her. I don't want the other girls to see me with her, and I won't take her hand. She doesn't look like a French-woman. What's more, she speaks with a foreign accent. When she's not speaking she keeps her mouth open the way foreigners do, like the refugees on the rue des Jardins Saint-Paul. That's where we live, at number 24. But across the street, at 35, almost no one speaks French. They're disgusting. As for me, I speak without an accent, like a real French girl. I was born in Paris, at the Hôtel-Dieu. Only I don't have a French name. When I'm called on in class I blush. The teacher can't pronounce my name. Everyone laughs. But I am not a foreigner. They say my name is German. But if the Germans question me they'll soon see that I'm really French. I look at my shoes, they're shining. I have to keep an eye on my doll in the box. One never knows in wartime; there're a lot of thieves, especially in train stations.

My mother is holding a paper bag. I recognize the smell of oranges—I know it's from the black market. I see grease stains through the paper. There must be some heavily buttered bread—it mustn't show—people mustn't know. I'm supposed to eat bread every day, and a lot of other nourishing things. But I won't eat unless I get a story. My mother tells me what's happening at the market. She tells me that they're cheating her. That makes me sad, but I want her to keep on talking. When she tells the same story twice, I stop eating. That gets on her nerves. She forces me but I clench my teeth. Then she cries and says I make her miserable. When she cries it makes me cry, too. I don't like to cry in front of people. My mother is always making me eat on the trains, in gardens, in the street, places where nobody eats.

I like stories and the street, too. Running in the street with a gang of little girls. They never come to my house. We swing on the chains around Ave Maria Square, across the street from the school where I'm learning to read. And then we run into the Métro Saint-Paul and push the buttons on the map that has all the different-colored lights. They chase us. We run away. I'm always the last and they shout at us, "You little brats!" We run back to St. Paul's Church, near the steps. I run faster. I'm afraid of churches. When the bells ring it's sad and grand. The great door is always closed, except for marriages. I love to see the bride in her white veil. I would like to get married like that when I'm big.

The stationmaster shouts and whistles—people rush around. I like the buttons on my new coat, I touch one of them through the buttonhole. For several evenings, my mother's been doing some sewing across the street at our neighbor's house, number 35. She also made some new dresses for my trip. And she left me all alone in the house. Locked in. I don't like to be locked in. I'm afraid my mother will be run over crossing the street and there'll be no one to open the door for me. She always leaves while I'm asleep, but I wake up; I scream and turn the light on in the blue room, which my mother painted all by herself. The last time I turned the light on I got very frightened. Someone yelled, "Light, third floor!" The Germans. I thought, It must be across the street, at number 35. I tried to open the door. I banged on it with my fists. You needed tools to open it. I saw the locksmith break one open once when I was at my nurse's in the country. I went to look for my father under the sideboard. My father—that's the toolbox. My mother says the tools are his and nobody's to touch them. I've never seen my father. He saw me when I was little. But I don't need him. According to my mother, he's traveling far away in Palestine. It's a hot country. When I eat figs—I don't like figs but they're nourishing—I think of him. They are fruits from over there. I also think of the old book that's on the toolbox. But I never say "my father" like other little girls; that seems funny to me. I'm not like them. My father is an engineer, that's very important. The old book is his, too. He knows how to read French. My mother doesn't. The beginning and end are

6

missing pages. But there are still a lot of them left hanging from threads. Rats have eaten it. Each time I look at the book, "It's serious," I say to myself. I sit on my little wooden stool and leaf through with the finger I put in my mouth, like I saw a very well-dressed lady do in the Tuileries gardens. I know the name of the book, but I always get up and go to my mother to ask her again. She says, "I've told you a thousand times, *The Wandering Jew*." My mother doesn't pay attention when I talk to her. She's always thinking of something else. I don't like to read alone. There are no pictures. I open the book again, sit down, and ask her once more what it says. She's busy, naked in the kitchen, washing herself in a basin. It's not nice; the French hide themselves when they wash.

It's strange, I think, that the Jews should be in a book. They have a book all to themselves. I picture them in the street and at number 35, talking Yiddish. It's not only rue des Jardins Saint-Paul. I think it over. I know that there are faraway things in the book which I don't know about. I repeat, "Wanderingjew, Wanderingjew"— Wandering is not part of his name, it doesn't sound Jewish.

We are Jews, too. Didn't want to say it before—got to be careful, you never know. But "nothing doing," it's like that. My mother always says "Nothing doing" when I insist and cry, she doesn't want to give me what I'm asking for. My family says I don't look it. But when I'm playing in the street I'm always afraid they're going to call me a Jew. That's why I don't want to be seen in the street with my mother except when she's wearing her nice navy-blue suit to go to the Tuileries gardens. My mother looks like a Jew. And often when I'm with the other girls I don't want them to come up to my house—I'm the first to say I don't like Jews, and everyone repeats it after me. Inside myself I feel uneasy. At home I'm Jewish. But in the street I could be French. But then, I have very curly hair. The teacher says it's pretty. All Jews have curly hair, that's how I recognize them. It's very important. Being with Jews is just like being at home; you can do what you want. But you've got to be careful when you are with French people. At our house we speak only Yiddish. Don't like Yiddish. I hate it when my mother talks it in the street or in the Métro with Aunt Ida. I'm ashamed. Don't dare tell my mother—she does it on purpose in the Métro; people look at us. I pinch her.

At home I don't care. I hear them talking in the kitchen in the morning, I go on sleeping. Aunt Ida comes more often now. They all say things aren't going well. There's a breeze in the room because my mother has opened the window, and you can hear the trucks in the street. I've got to get up to go to school. I don't want to get up. My mother calls me. And then she goes on talking to my aunt. That puts me to sleep. I'd like to sleep like that for a long time, without ever waking up and with them always talking. I also hear "Ve gotta hide" all the time. Everybody at our house goes around saying we have to hide. Touching and squeezing my mother's curls at night when I'm in bed or in her arms; that puts me to sleep, too, and I close my eyes. But the curls always spring back again. She has pretty curly hair like me. Only she doesn't have time to comb it because she has to work a lot in order to get permit papers.

The neighbors come every day now to Adolphe's, on the second floor, to get papers. Adolphe is a big boy.

8

He's sixteen and very wise. He draws on a big tilted table that has a lamp, and he turns a fat needle around on his notebook with a pencil. He's making circles. He's serious. His mother says that he works and is going to be an engineer. It's a good profession. My mother and I often go there for papers. They say he understands all about these things. Afterward, we'll have to go to City Hall; maybe they'll change our name. Adolphe knows everything; he tells us in Yiddish how to fix everything. Things are becoming difficult. Everyone wants to leave. He, Adolphe, has an agreement with the concierge. She's a real Frenchwoman. I'm leaving, too, but not because of that. *I* am French. I don't put on an act with Adolphe and they say I'm getting some sense at last, that I'm changing. They laugh, that astonishes them. When I grow up I'm going to marry him. Only my mother's going to have to pay a fine for the light. She didn't put up the blackout curtain. That was us on the third floor. My mother's waiting downstairs to pay; I don't dare go home. She puts her hand under her chin when she's thinking. Because of me, she owes a lot of money. Adolphe couldn't fix that. He said my mother has a lot of worries, she goes to a lot of trouble for me. And also that I'm a difficult child, have to find a place to send me.

I'm afraid Adolphe will find the bubble gum that I stick to the corner of the staircase; near the coal cellar, it's all dark. I pick it up in the street, people throw it away. My mother doesn't like me to chew it and won't buy it for me. You can find it by the sidewalk where there are little gutters with pieces of paper, colored bottles, and peelings. I look at the ground. My mother says, "Why do you always walk with your head down?"

I'm looking for things. My mother calls them filthy. I never find money. I also chew bubble gum in the street and stick it downstairs before going up. But I can't make balloons and bubbles with my mouth like the other little girls. They say that I'm dumb and won't show me how they do it. I try to make some all alone by the chains of Ave Maria Square across from school, because I'm waiting for a little girl. She promised to show me her mechanical doll if I let her wear the wristwatch my mother just bought me while she went to get it. She didn't come back. I waited till dark. The poor people had already finished standing in line for the soup kitchen. I didn't tell my mother right away. She had come to look for me. I was afraid. She said it didn't matter, the watch didn't work. I had believed it was a real watch like hers. Aunt Ida said the little girl had had me and that the next time I gotta be less trusting. Mustn't believe people.

The Red Cross lady helps the girls to get on the train. My mother pushes me up the steps by the behind. I don't like that. I know you mustn't touch the rail, you get black on your hands. While I'm climbing up I look at the little girl's black stockings and her short dress and garters, and the panties underneath. It's nice. My mother always makes me long dresses because of the cold. I look at my legs; my socks are held up at the knees by rubber bands, but they're always falling down because I have legs like drumsticks, my nurse says, and I'm thin. My mother said, "Nothing doing," for the long black stockings. She didn't put any in the bag that she packed and labeled for my trip.

My mother may have hugged and kissed me when we parted. I don't remember, I was in a hurry to leave. Later I learned that all mothers cry and little girls, too, when they part. Maybe she cried; I seem to remember that I didn't look at her. I felt rid of her and of rue des Jardins Saint-Paul. Finally, everything was going to be new. The train was leaving.

I lost my ration card with all the tickets for the school cafeteria. We also used to buy milk with it, at the rue Saint-Paul dairy shop. The shopkeeper would measure the milk out and pour it, and you could see her fingers all swollen with chilblains beyond where her gloves were cut off in the middle of her hand. Only little girls have a right to more food with ration cards.

I'm growing up and I have to get dressed all by myself. Every morning I tell my mother that tomorrow I'm going to dress myself. When my mother puts my socks on she tickles my feet to warm them. I always have cold feet. She says they're big and there's no time to buy me new shoes, that they are already too small. It's not nice for a little girl to have big feet, Aunt Ida says. I don't want to grow any bigger.

The train whistles; smoke is blurring everything. The little girls are seated next to the Red Cross lady, who took my package of provisions and is giving out buttered bread and oranges. I watch them eat. It all belongs to my mother; they don't know it; it all belongs to me and I'm the only one with things from the black market. I refuse the bread and butter the lady offers me. I like to see them eat; that way, there'll be more for them. I'm all by myself on my seat. The string around the shoebox with my doll is dangling from the luggage rack. The train is swallowing up the landscape and you can't see the big houses anymore. We're somewhere else. That's the end of rue des Jardins Saint-Paul!

One of the little girls has fallen asleep. I look at the shine on my shoes. I'd like to speak to the girl who's awake. Maybe she has a doll, too; if not, I'll let her play with mine. She has straight hair with neat bangs and a white ribbon tied in the middle in a bow, just like real French girls who have pretty mammas who whisper. I saw some, Sunday at the Tuileries gardens, when I was walking with my mother. There are fine ladies with large hats, and little boys wearing patent-leather shoes right by the pond where the little sailboats float. You can also see white statues upside down in the water, and they quiver between the trees.

One day I was standing next to a lady while my mother was sitting on a bench. I was watching the little boats sail by; one had come right up to the edge. I thought of the song about the "little ship" that I had learned at school "that had never sailed before" and "the sailors at sea." The little boy was using a stick to hold it back. I put my hand out and touched the sail with my finger. I saw my hand in the water, too. The lady suddenly turned around and said, batting her eyelashes, "You rude child!" She had long legs that touched each other everywhere and you could see them quivering on the water in a zigzag. She'd taken the little boy by one hand and, with her other hand, was holding the boat, which was dripping on the gravel. I followed her and looked at her legs, which were making noise because they were rubbing against each other in her narrow skirt. I made noise, too, dragging my feet. When I'm big I'm going to walk like her.

12

. . .

We're still on the train. The Red Cross lady pulls the dress down over the knees of the little girl who's asleep; one mustn't see her panties. And then she brushes back a lock of hair from her forehead. Her hair is completely straight. She's a real French girl. I'd like the lady to do something for me, too. I'm sitting across from her, and the oranges and bread are all gone.

Léa, the shoemaker's daughter next door, used to get oranges from me, too. I used to take them to her, but in return for something else—we had an agreement. It was only chocolate and oranges that my mother would allow me to eat out in the street. I would throw the chocolate bar behind the little stove on our landing, and hide the orange under my smock, held up by my belt. I was careful because once I'd bought some little celluloid dolls with money I'd taken from my mother and had hidden them under my smock, but while I was running they fell out on the street, all of them! Anyway, I was running to Léa's. It was agreed that she would let me play with her dolls and pieces of cloth. My mother rushed over on the landing to catch me. "Don't let anyone see you!" But I was already in the street when I heard her opening the window; I was passing number 35 and turning the corner—in front of the statue of the little boy peeing in the basin. Across from the bistro where the French drink wine you come to a demolished house, all open, with no door, with pillars. Like the one at Berck Beach, where we lived in a cloth shack because of my weak legs; the doctor'd said I needed sea air. Léa lives upstairs; there's no hallway, you can see everything. I'd walk in the sand, it got in my shoes. I found foil paper and wire. Léa is always alone in the

13

house. She has eight older brothers and sisters, but they're never there. Her father and mother work somewhere else, so we can do whatever we want. As soon as I arrive she says, "You give me first!" I give her the orange from under my smock. I promise her some bread and butter for next time and rush toward the big chest crammed with scraps of cloth, large dolls, and the little celluloid ones. Their arms and legs have all come off, but you can reattach them with shoemaker's thread. If you rummage carefully you can find something: boxes and shiny buttons; there are usually scraps of cloth. And then there are things all over the house lying on the table and in the kitchen. It's not like at home. But it's no fun searching alone. Léa is busy with the bottles and little jars; she doesn't want to show them to me in case I let out the flies trapped inside the jar and they fly away. I know she collects them from the garbage cans at number 35, where you find them in all colors.

It's slow, the train keeps moving; I'm yawning and I'm in a hurry to get there. Now the other little girl is sleeping, too. *I* only sleep at night when I touch my mother's curls.

The French drink a lot of wine and eat Camembert with a penknife, and they get drunk. My mother says it's unwholesome and I should be careful when I see them on the street. They zigzag when they walk and are brutes. Right in front of Léa's house there's a bistro that smells of wine and cigarettes. The men have caps. I run fast when I pass it; they swear and sing very loudly.

Once, I saw some people from the neighborhood gathered in front of the statue of the little boy who's peeing. They were looking at a Frenchman who was wearing a cap and moving forward on one leg; the other was only the leg of his pants held up by a safety pin. He was trying to climb up the base. His crutches were on the bench. The people were saying he was a Frenchman from the war of 1914. He was clinging to some protruding edges; you could see his pants leg with the safety pin flapping in the air, and no one was stopping him—it was funny. He looked happy and was singing, "A flower in your hat, a song on your lips, a heart joyous and sincere . . ." At the top of the statue he stood up straight, searched his pocket, and flung some coins, which came raining down all over the ground. Everybody rushed to pick them up, jostling each other, as he took up his song again: ". . . and it's all you need to go to the ends of the earth." I didn't take any coins. I wanted to but it was too late. There were none left. I'm not quick. We waited and looked up so that he would throw some more. Which he did. Then, I rushed forward and quickly scooped up everything I could. It was the first time I'd ever found money in the street. I ran to rue Charlemagne before my mother could catch me, to the school store, and asked for some cachous and bubble gum. The lady gave me some and counted the money. I was afraid she'd discover it wasn't real and I was astonished. I went back to the place near the statue, but there was no one there anymore. I hummed, "To go to the ends of the earth," and looked on the ground, but all I saw was a safety pin.

It's tiring to watch the poles from the train all the time. You think the wires are going to get tangled, but they always come straight again; it makes you blink.

15

You can see the fields through them. The wires move up and down with the train, birds are flying off. It's like the song about the emperor and the little prince who comes back every day "to shake hands." It never changes. You'd like to stop but you can't. I don't believe in a whole week of Sundays.

The train grates, slows down, and stops. I stand at the window and look at the little girls in their red-and-white-check uniforms and their berets, in line all down the platform. The nuns are waiting nearby. I saw them first because of their coifs like big birds' wings. Now you can see the folds of their long blue robes and the smooth white bibs over their chests. The little girls' heads pop out of the compartment doors; the train is full and soon I'll see them running out. The sisters stop them and line them up. They have wide sleeves. They're the same ones I saw at the school dispensary when I went for my checkup. The little girls are laughing and being noisy, but they quiet down once they're in line. Nobody has a doll. I take a closer look; they're all older than me. I climb back into the compartment, take my doll out of the shoebox, and with one blow, without looking, send the box, string and all, flying to the rails. It gives me a dizzy feeling in my stomach, the way I felt at home when I threw eggshells out the window: I was afraid to look. I felt as though I were falling with them on the head of some passerby. I ran straight to the kitchen and my mother asked, "What have you done now!" I shut my eyes a minute; the shoebox is going to be crushed by a train. A little boy in our neighborhood was run over by a German truck and they said he was crushed.

. . .

We are walking in line, a nice straight line, in the sun. We have to keep step, avoid the heels of those in front of us and not spoil the nice line. I can see the whole line because I'm last. I look down at my feet; that makes them look tangled. Our group moves toward the village. The sisters, on either side of us, take big strides. Their long robes widen at the bottom; the pleats open and reform again over their heels, like the long trains you see in fairy-tale illustrations. Their shoes are flat, their hands are crossed and hidden in their wide sleeves. You hear the clicking of the string of big beads that ends in a cross at the hem of their robes. To keep them from falling off, I think. The way in school, when we were stringing necklaces, we would moisten the thread in order to make a knot. Mine would never hold. The beads would slip off. I never managed to make a necklace. The beads are shining in the sun and the little crosses are tossing about. The sisters push us toward the sidewalk because a hay cart is coming. They are talking softly, whispering. You can hardly hear them. I would like to go nearer but I mustn't break up the nice line. We begin to sing, "A sacred flame rises from our native soil, Marshal Pétain; here we are before you, France's savior . . ." I sing very loudly, saying all the words. It's a song I learned at school, at Christmas, when they were giving out our gifts: sketchbooks and colored pencils from the Marshal. We are his children; we are the children of France. Our teacher also said that we are hope and that our country will be reborn. It's in the song. Behind her desk was a picture of the Marshal with a mustache.

Some peasants stop to look at us. I wish we'd sing louder and stronger; we are from Paris. Here it smells of horse dung and manure and you see puddles and ducks. Every time I leave Paris there's the same smells. The houses are all low. You can't see any cars; people walk.

My doll's a nuisance; if only she could walk! We're already at the end of the village; we're skirting a stone wall below some large trees. We turn in order to go through a high iron gate with golden spikes. Now we see great green lawns. At the end of the broad, unpaved Avenue where we're walking is a château—a real one. You'd think it was the manor house of Lorris, where my mother and I were refugees in the free zone. Every day we used to go to the pond near the tall trees, the birds, and no people. It was so quiet—we were all alone. I was in a bathing suit near a stream and I would block the current with my fingers. My mother would sit on the grass and do mending for the lady of the manor. There was a little boy on her knees; I thought he was my brother. We even have a photo of it.

Still in line, we arrive in front of the château. We're not singing anymore. All we hear is the noise of the gravel under our feet. The façade looks like the row of big arcades and columns on the rue de Rivoli. One of the old students says, "It's the refectory." She shows us the park and we walk through it along the broad, tree-lined Avenue. Her name is Thérèse and she's wearing a little cross at the end of a thin gold chain. She also shows us a big statue in the middle of the lawn. It's the Sacred Heart. It's surrounded by climbing roses and is tearing its clothes with both hands in the place where rays are coming out of its heart, like a drawing of the sun.

We enter the refectory through a large door. The old

students, in uniform, go first and make a slight bow to Sister Marie, who is holding the swinging door. The girls take their place in front of little numbered napkin holders and tin plates. I also incline my head before Sister Marie. Her coif is stiffer than those of the other sisters; her face is bony, her hands, too. She has hardly any eyebrows; they're very blond and you can't see her hair, even through the gap in her coif. The old students say that she's very strict.

We're all standing, with the bench right against our knees. I'd like to sit down, but we turn toward the statue of a lady in a pleated robe set between two jars of flowers on a large mantelpiece. She holds her hands open at each side of her gown, which is neatly draped with a belt at the waist, and she seems so gentle and kind in her long veil. It's for her we're singing, I think. We all raise our hands and touch our foreheads and shoulders. I watch what the others are doing: I make a circle around my face.

Mademoiselle Laure gives us each a soup bowl—she's a peasant from Beaujeu. All you hear is the sound of spoons. Mademoiselle Janine carries the big steaming pots back to the kitchen. Whenever we talk too much Sister Marie goes "Shush, shush . . . silence, mesdemoiselles." Everyone quiets down. I myself don't say a word. Even in Paris when I knew the names of the little girls at school they didn't talk to me; maybe it's because they knew my mother wasn't French. I can't finish my pumpkin soup; it's a nice yellow color and when you stir it with your spoon it makes waves. Sister Marie announces that we have to finish everything on our plates. I look at the Marshal on the wall; it's him again, the same man with the mustache. If I turn around I can see the Sacred Heart through the window, among the roses.

I'm with the juniors. They divided us up into junior, intermediate, and senior students. There're a lot of dormitories; you get to them by shiny, polished corridors. Sister says there are more of us now because of the war. We each have a bed with a little table next to it. I stuff my doll into the back. I'll look at her at night when everyone's asleep. The old students fold their bedspreads. There's a big pail with a lid in the middle of the dormitory for going to the toilet. At first I wait to see what the others do. The girl next to me, Thérèse, folds her clothes as soon as she takes them off and lays them at the foot of her bed; she smooths all the folds and doesn't take off her panties until she's put on her nightgown. How clever!—you can't see a thing. Then she opens her bedside table and looks at pictures. I go nearer. She says, "Holy pictures." They're pretty. I ask her to lend me some. The people have circles of light over their heads; they have bare feet and long hair. I also see a naked man on a cross; he has a piece of cloth between his legs—he's the same as the man on the cross hanging on the dormitory wall. Thérèse takes her pictures back. She says, "I'm going to pray," and she kneels in front of her bed, clasping her hands with her fingers crossed. She prays. It's lovely. I'd like to learn. Then she lifts her eyes to the ceiling. I do the same, but all I see are lights; there are three. The other little girls are kneeling next to the beds in their nightgowns. They're very serious and lower their heads. You'd think they were unhappy or were crying, hiding their faces in their hands. Maybe they're just telling secrets, by moving their lips. At my old school we used to whisper in people's ears. I don't have any secrets. When they make the sign with the hand, I know it's finished. Several of them are already in bed, Thérèse too. Sister Marie comes over, tucks her in, and kisses her on the forehead. She says, "Good night, my child."

Someone says, "Sister, Jacqueline's crying!" Sister Marie goes over to her. You can't hear; she's crying very softly. She wants her mamma; everyone's looking at her. Jacqueline is still dressed in her pretty yellow open-work blouse. I'd seen her at the station jumping rope. Sister is standing very close, stroking her hair and saying, "You'll see Mamma soon, darling!" But that only makes her cry more. She's holding a white hand-kerchief with a lace border and blowing her nose. She's very sad and her eyes are red; it's nice. *I* am unable to cry; I snivel, my nurse says, and make a lot of noise. Once, when I was crying, I even looked at myself in the mirror. My mother cries quietly, too. She gets upset because of me. Maybe when I grow up I'll be sad with red eyes.

Sister turns the lights off, all except the night light. She closes the double door and says, "May God be with you, my children."

I can't get to sleep and twist my neck because of the roll under my head—it's a bolster, we don't have pillows. And I don't have my mother's curls. I try to make the sign with my hand under the sheets. I say, "In the name of the Father," that's the forehead . . . After that you have to touch your stomach and bring your hand back up to each shoulder. I can't sing it, everyone's sleeping. I hear the noise of the train and I see the poles and wires and the Red Cross lady. I lean on my elbows and look at the three rows of beds and the heads sticking out above the sheets. It's very quiet. I get up, the floor creaks under my bare feet. The night light casts a circle on the pail. I don't dare lift the lid—that will make a noise. I touch the feet of the statue with the baby, and the folds of her long stone robe. They feel cold. She's wearing a golden crown like the queens. All the shoes have been placed at the bottom of the beds, like an avenue of shoes. Suddenly the shadow moves; the curtains edge forward in the dark. I'm afraid. Maybe it's a ghost or the sandman. I run to my bed. Thérèse stirs and murmurs something with a sigh. My sheets are cold.

"Everyone up!" Sister Marie pulls back my covers. Everyone gets up. The covers have been pulled back to the foot of each bed. Thérèse is already dressed. Some little girls with white towels over their shoulders are standing in line in front of one of the open windows. Mademoiselle Laure runs a fine-tooth comb through their hair, looking for lice. She traps them between the teeth of the comb and crushes them with her thumbnail. I see one fall on the towel, he's running; she crushes him and it makes a bloodstain. They comb *my* hair separately, with a wide-tooth comb, because I have beautiful curly hair and a fine comb won't pass. One of the seniors, who comes to help the little ones get ready in the morning, makes me some ringlets. Another one comes over and makes them for me on the other side. Everyone is looking at me and saying what beautiful hair I have. I feel proud. All the other girls have straight hair. Sister Marie enters the line with scissors and clippers. Martine has long hair rolled up in tight curlers in front. She lifts her hands and cries, "I don't want it cut!" Sister Marie grabs her and slaps her. She cries silently. We look at her. That will teach her to disobey!

Each girl has her own faucet and toothbrush. We wash our faces in the corridor with washcloths. Everyone hurries. I watch how they put the toothpaste on; mine isn't the same. "Come on, come on, what are you dreaming about? Stop dawdling!" says Sister Marie, and she picks up my towel, which has fallen in the water.

We go to Mass carrying books. We go down some very wide stairs with gold-colored banisters. You can see, through the big windows, white lilac and ivy growing over the wall. We are lined up according to height. We cross a lot of corridors. Sister says, "This is the way you must walk when you go to chapel."

The rotunda is full of statues and cabinets with big books. We put on our uniforms there. The new girls will get theirs this afternoon. The entire sacristy wall is one large mirror, but we pass in front of it without looking at ourselves; the parquet shines. There's also a very large wooden cross; you see the man attached all white with a red spot on his side. I recognize the smell of the church; it gives me a chilly feeling. But here it's heated. I'm not afraid as I was in Paris and Lorris—I'm big now.

In Lorris when you went to school you had to pass beside the church in front of a big stone wall; you didn't see any windows, nobody went there, only the wind. I was lucky, I could go back another way, I would go at noon with a girl friend straight to the Germans. They'd arrived a few days before, and at noon you could eat buttered noodles in their mess hall. My mother found out about it and forbade me to go, but not really, because I ate well there—I even gained weight—and also because I said that the Germans were giving noodles to the poor and everyone came there to eat. I had a friend, a nice soldier. I was only scared of him when he put his steel helmet on his head. My girl friend had a friend, too. We would go to see them after class, at the boys' school, in the big square they requisitioned the night they arrived with tanks and cannons. My friend would even sing to me in German; he'd sit me on his lap, everyone would laugh, and we'd leave in a truck to go to the pond at the manor. Once, I went into the boys' school, into the big hall; all the soldiers were sleeping on the floor with their heads on their sacks and guns. I went up to my friend; he was sleeping, too. I wanted to have some fun with him and I took away the sack from under his head. He woke up all red, looking angry. I was very frightened and ran away. He almost caught me; he wanted to hit me and was holding the knife that he always kept by his side. The other soldiers grabbed his arms and stopped him. I haven't gone back to the mess hall since. And I had to go home from school running by way of the church.

I know that the priest lives there; he's all black, in a long gown with lots of little buttons in front. He's very polite and always smiles. Once, my mother and I went into the church through the big door, with a neighbor. She knelt down near a table with lots of short lighted candles. We, my mother and I, stayed in the aisle and didn't do anything. We never do the same things as other people. I moved my foot and the sound continued for a long time. I also said, "Ouh, ouhou ahah . . ." The echo came back from everywhere. My mother put her hand over my mouth. I wanted to light some candles. My mother said it was stupid. But *I* know that all French people go to church. They bury their dead there.

We enter the chapel through two pretty doors with pictures set in them. We stop to dip our hands in a basin with angels around it and then cross ourselves. When it's my turn I put my hand in. I wet my sleeve and the carpet, making the sign; some drops trickle onto my arm. But I don't make a sound. The sisters say you mustn't make a sound.

The chapel is very pretty; it's full of colors, statues, and objects that are new to me. There are pictures with lights and flowers on the wall. And tall candles. We kneel before a wooden rail on a raised carpet in the middle of one of the aisles—but only on one knee. The other stays bent on the floor. You have to be careful not to fall. I see Martine in front of me; she's doing very well at making the sign of the cross, only her sock has slipped down to her ankle and she hasn't pulled it up. It's forbidden. Behind the rail there're some steps with fringed carpets and tables covered with white cloths and pretty gold boxes. The old-timers have places to sit on the benches. But we kneel on a little step. It hurts. After a minute you get used to it. We all cross our hands on the support and wait with the book.

When the priest enters, we stand up. He's wearing the same black gown and also a white lace shirt, but you can still see the little buttons, on the bottom of the gown. He leans over a big book and speaks very fast in a foreign language. Everybody answers him and follows in the book. Sometimes he turns around and stretches out his arms on both sides and afterward begins again. We sing in the foreign language, too. The priest is silent, he just gestures. I didn't learn this song at school. Or at the public baths my mother and I used to go to in Paris where I learned songs, one about Marie: "Marie Tournelle is the loveliest of all in the evening, hear her sing . . ." Here, only one group sings, near the little piano where the sister is playing with one hand and beating time with the other. They sing in parts. It's very pretty. Nobody moves or makes a sound.

Thérèse gets up and the others walk behind her in a line toward the rail, where they kneel; the priest takes some little white disks out of a gold vase and puts them in their mouths. They don't eat it; maybe they swallow it. They look sad as they go back to their places; they hide their faces in their hands. Sometimes we sit down, too. I don't know who's giving the signal and I copy the others, but a little behind, so I'm always the last. I feel like yawning, but I stop myself. How good the flowers and wax smell!

At the sound of the little bell I think it's over. It's Sister Marie ringing; she's kneeling on a low, straw-bottomed chair. The folds of her long robe fall around it and you see only her heels. The sisters are all on one side, kneeling on the straw-bottomed chairs. Maybe they hurt less than wood. It's silent. They all put their heads in their hands now. I peek through my fingers to see what you're supposed to do afterward. We begin a French song: "One day I'll go to see her in the heavens of my homeland . . ." The girl next to me follows the words in the book. It's written: "Hymn for the Virgin." We sing softly. At school we used to shout. The group of singers is standing around the little piano now. They're lucky. "In the heavens, in the heavens . . . yes,

I will go to see Ma-ry!"—they repeat in unison. The priest leaves by the sacristy. Mass is over.

At breakfast, we tear off bits of bread and drop them in our bowls of coffee; they float around and we catch them with our spoons. I already know how to say grace by heart and I make the sign of the cross. You have to eat politely and hold your hand on the table and not bother the person next to you. Sister supervises us. You mustn't open your mouth too much. It's forbidden to talk. All the little girls know these things. There're also lots of other manners they've learned that we don't practice at home.

They know the answers to all the questions in catechism, the ones in big letters and even the ones in fine print. We're all sitting under the chestnut tree, on the benches arranged in a square beside the lawn. Our arms are crossed and the catechism is on our knees. Sister Anne is in the middle on a chair and only her shoes show under her robe. She marks the pages of the catechism that have holy pictures. She talks about the Scriptures. She tells us about the Good Lord, about Jesus Christ, His son.

The Lord preached in Jerusalem. His mother was in Nazareth. She was sad because he'd left but he was the Son of God and had to obey. He never changed his clothes. His clothing grew with him from birth. It was a miracle because he had grace. Later he studied in the temple, among the Pharisees and the fowl, because they dealt in the market. I know, they were Jews. My mother dealt in the market, too, in Paris. The Holy Virgin had grace; she was holy. Bernadette of Lourdes, too. She was a virgin; she crossed a stream. She put her bare feet in the water and they didn't get wet. What's more, she was sickly, she had asthma—and she was cured. It was a miracle.

The Blessed Virgin appeared to her. It was because she was pure and her soul was white, spotless. Poor thing, she was only fourteen. People didn't believe her. Man is unbelieving. The world is full of pagans—wayward souls who don't believe in the Trinity. They're going to be miserable in the next world because of their ignorance. But the Christian path is open to them to render glory to God.

You can see, in the distance, the trees around the park lawn and the statue of the Sacred Heart in the middle. God is everywhere—especially in heaven. When you pray, you look up. I wonder if Bernadette is also the Blessed Virgin. But I don't dare ask. They'd make fun of me. Everyone knows, because no one asks anything. You have to listen. Besides, I'm not completely Christian yet. But now I know that if you have the will you can convert, and God is very good.

I think about it while we're taking our walk in the park along the big Avenue that begins at the enclosed courtyard. We pass a little bridge over a moat. But there's no water, only stones and grass. Maybe I could try a stream, to see if my feet stay dry in the water like St. Bernadette's. You can barely see the sky under the big trees; the light comes from the sun between the leaves. Two of the old students take Sister Marie's arm. The girls next to them join hands and move forward in a group. I follow them and watch them walk. We pass the Circle, where the four paths meet; it's the playing field. There're some small stone benches around it with mossy feet. I find an empty snail shell on one of them and throw it as far as I can. The little girls tell Sister Marie stories and we're all listening as we walk. Madeleine speaks with an accent. She is from Dijon. She rolls her r's. Geneviève is from Brittany. She has very thin legs like me. When we come to the little grotto we stop a minute to hail the Virgin Mary. It reminds me of the old Gallic cave that I saw at school in an illustration, with Vercingetorix, a little room with no doors or windows. The Virgin Mary is standing at the entrance because it's dark inside; she's wearing a pretty dress with a blue belt and stars. The other end of the park is like a big field. We separate and set out to pick cornflowers in front of St. Joseph's oratory; you can see our château in the distance. Joseph is old and has a beard; he's standing in the middle of the columns. We pass by without praying to St. Joseph. He's only the father by adoption. He's not God's father.

One of the little girls tells a story. She has a Dijon accent, too. I can never tell stories. We Parisians outnumber the others and we're proud. Also, I prefer a Parisian accent. But whenever I hear a girl from Dijon talking, I can't help rolling my r's like her. I lose my own accent.

After lunch we take our naps on canvas cots. It's for our lungs. Each girl takes a cot and we line them up in straight rows under the lindens. It's very boring to lie down like that for so long. You can't have any fun, you're not allowed to speak or move. You have a long time to think about the saints and the Trinity. Mademoiselle Laure—she's from Beaujeu—is in charge. Her hand is wrapped in a sock because she's darning our clothes. She keeps a pair of scissors in her smock, and a rosary, because she's devout. She also has two chins when she laughs. The other girls all fall asleep immediately. I tell myself stories. I'm in Haute-Saône. A linden leaf has fallen down my neck. I take it. "Mademoiselle," Laure cries. "You over there! Fidgeting all the time!" I stop fidgeting. I think of the daughters in the church and of the world full of pagans. I'm not a pagan anymore. I'm learning my catechism.

In the refectory, Sister Marie announces that the new girls are to assemble in the sacristy after the Angelus. They have to examine our papers. The priest is expecting us.

I don't look in the sacristy mirror anymore—that's vanity; I want to be humble. I resist the temptation. I look at the big picture of the Pope, it's Pius XII surrounded by cardinals. They rank beneath the pontiff, our Head. We enter the parlor, where the priest is sitting. He's going through the files, examining our papers—and an especially important one, the baptismal certificate. He holds a black notebook and jots down our names. His hand trembles as he writes; the veins are swollen into green tubes and you can see little red threads in his blue eyes. Also, he has skin hanging from his chin. And it jiggles when he talks. But he doesn't talk to us. Except at Mass, covered in a chasuble, and then you can barely see his face because he keeps it turned toward the altar and is leaning over his big missal. He speaks to God in Latin. When he turns around, his arm stretched out, to bless us, the skin under his chin moves even more. He speaks fast and has a lot of spit in his mouth. That's because of the Latin. It hurts your throat when you speak Latin. Except when you sing; the Latin hymns are very pretty. And I'm even beginning to understand the words,: I already know them by heart. They sound more devout in Latin and I can think about the Good Lord from the bottom of my heart with the right words.

Our parish priest is very old, he's eighty-two. He's Alsatian, proud and courageous because of Alsace-Lorraine. All the people from there are proud and courageous because of the Germans. It says so in the songs the little girls taught me; one of them is very pretty and sad. It's about a beggar girl who refuses money from a German soldier because she's proud; she says to him, "Keep your gold, I will keep my suffering; to Germans will I never offer my hand because I am a child of France . . ."

Mademoiselle Eugénie, the lady who takes care of Father Boildou, says he is a saintly man. They live in a little house set apart, near the pink pavilion. She wears a white wig and glasses. A pinhead has got stuck under the skin of her hand, near her thumb. They have a nice garden with big pots with angels and lots of roses. From their house on the hill you see fields and the houses in Beaujeu, with the pointed church in the middle. Inside, it smells of incense; it's very dark, with lots of furniture and pictures of saints.

The priest knows that almost all the girls are baptized. They even say their godfathers' and godmothers' names as they curtsy to him, and he registers them in a notebook. He didn't ask anything when it was my turn. Alice says they ate a lot of sugar-coated almonds at her ceremony. They all have a baptismal certificate. I myself have nothing but a paper from the dispensary saying I have a spot on my lungs. I also have spotty freckles, but it's the spot on one's soul that counts. We have to erase our ancestors' original sin. The little girls show off their chains and gold crosses, proof of their baptism. Sister Marie has come, too. She's the one who looks at my papers. She's strict. She says, "We'll write to your mother to ask for authorization." I want to tell her that it's no use, my mother speaks Yiddish, she's Jewish. One mustn't ask her, it's no concern of hers. We're different. Those things aren't important to us. Being well fed and warmly dressed, that's all that matters. But I don't say anything, I keep quiet around French people. Secretly I think, Maybe my mother has been "taken away." In rue des Jardins Saint-Paul, they used to say, when people left, "They've been taken away."

Wednesdays we have potatoes in their skins—in their jackets, it's called—a couple of salad leaves, and a little pat of butter. You can remove the skin by scratching it off with your finger—it's like paper—and then you can stick it onto the tin plate. It's a mess plate. When you touch it with your fork it makes a sound like the little Angelus bell. Sister Marie scolds: "Stop this commotion, please!" If you eat the butter with your potato, there's none left for the bread. Germaine saves hers for the crust; she eats the inside of the potato separately. There're some drops of oil on the salad leaf, I touch it and make it quiver; a drop spills onto the plate, like Jacqueline's tears. Between the pots on the table, Mademoiselle Laure is ladling out some stewed gooseberries. We wait, it's a good dessert, everyone likes it. Mademoiselle Laure drips some of the juice on the brown package. It's neatly done up with strings, the way my mother used to wrap packages at home in Paris. I used to watch her pressing her finger and pulling tight. I'd offer to help, but she'd get annoyed.

After dessert they give us our letters. They say, "Here's the mail!" We all wait, our arms crossed. Everyone hopes for a letter. It's very important to get letters from your parents. We watch the girls who get letters as they read. We're envious. They read and re-read them and then put them away in their lockers in the courtyard. They don't let anyone see because you've got to mind your own business. I myself haven't re-ceived any letters yet. Germaine has had two. One was in a pretty pink envelope with a gray lining. "Made-moiselle F." Sister Marie is calling me. I'm scared and feel my neck and cheeks growing hot. She looks at me. "Come here!" And she beckons. There's total si-lence. I unfasten the napkin around my neck and climb over the bench, my foot bumping Germaine; I wonder what I could have done. "Hurry up, there's a package for you!" People are whispering, the package is mine. I recognize my mother's knots and the way she ties the string. Sister Marie removes the scissors tied to the ribbon on her rosary and cuts the string. You can open without cutting. I know how to undo knots. Inside a big box I see a pair of espadrilles—my mother had promised them to me—a jump rope, some fruit, a little suitcase, and some other things; Sister Marie touches them. "I hope, mademoiselle, that you are not going to keep these good things all to yourself; remember your neighbor and be charitable." I bow my head. "Yes, Sister." I return to my seat, the package in my arms. All over the room, the girls are leaning over their tables to look.

Germaine, she's an old student, says that no one has ever received such a big package before. It's fantastic! I can't stop my mind wandering as we're singing grace—you're supposed to think about what you're saying in your prayer to God. But I keep seeing the little suitcase and the espadrilles for gym; let's hope they're not too big, my mother always buys them too big because I grow so fast and they're expensive.

Germaine, Thérèse, and some other little girls follow me to the courtyard. I'm going to put my things in my locker. I still have nothing in it except for three holy pictures and a rosary. It's the priest who gave them to me. He stroked my hair and said, "Make good use of them, my child," because I haven't been baptized yet and I need grace. The old students' lockers are filled with little things wrapped in fine paper in nice boxes. They open them just a tiny bit, so you can't see in. One of them said to me, "None o' your business!" I wanted to see what was in the package first, because it was from my mother. But they followed me because of "love thy neighbor." I was already on my way when I put the package down and gave them all the chocolate. The only thing I kept was the paper with the hazelnut design. They went on looking at me and I gave them the candy. I put the wrapping paper in my locker. What a pity! The stamps that say "Beaujeu, Haute-Saône" are torn. I roll the string into a little ball, like my mother. I try on the espadrilles; all the girls are looking at me. I lace them. The others are standing around eating my things. Tomorrow there'll be nothing left. I also wanted two tennis balls to bat against the wall. I'll write my mother on correspondence day.

. . .

It's Thursday, the day for writing letters and also for reading; we read by ourselves. They push the benches against the wall in the refectory. We write our parents on some paper they give us. Those of us who have nothing to write read the lives of the saints. All the books about saints are covered in blue paper with labels and are stacked on Sister Marie's desk. She watches us from her desk. I am writing my mother to ask her for things. It's the first time I've ever written a letter. My lines are crooked, I've drawn five. Afterward I have nothing left to ask for. I watch Claudine; she applies herself as though it were schoolwork, bending over with her tongue sticking out between her lips. She fills a long page, then turns it over. I'd like to see how she writes, but she hides the page with her hand. I've finished my letter and take it up to Sister Marie's desk. I choose *The Life of St. Guy* to read on the bench.

Little Guy is very ill but he's a good boy and offers his suffering to little Jesus. He makes sacrifices. He knows that he's going to die soon. His father and mother are very very sad. But he is not afraid of his earthly end. He is pure and will go to heaven. He's a good Christian.

"Mademoiselle F., come here!" I walk toward the table near Sister Marie. She puts the letters in envelopes. Mine is on top. She hasn't called anyone else yet. "Mademoiselle, this is not the way one writes a letter to one's mamma. You're an ungrateful, slovenly child!" She's holding my letter; I see another one underneath written in ink with straight lines and pretty slanted letters. "Mademoiselle S." That's my last name—it's serious when they call you by your last name. "First of all, one begins by thanking one's mamma. Then one inquires about her health. It's only in closing that one politely asks, 'My dear mamma, can you send me some scissors?' "

It's scissors with bone handles I've asked for; my mother promised them to me, and also a lace petticoat and a sewing box. Sister Marie continues, "No one else has written as rude a letter as you." I thought of telling her that it was Adolphe who reads and writes the letters. My mother never writes, she hasn't time. She'll ask Adolphe what I want—that's what really matters. My mother is different. She doesn't care about manners. But I don't say anything. Sister Marie doesn't know and one must not be rude. I have to rewrite the letter. It's very annoying to write a letter when you can't ask for the things you need.

We'd returned all the books and put the tables and benches back in place in order to get ready for vespers. We put our uniforms on in the rotunda. I think of St. Guy. I haven't finished his life. He was going to die and go to heaven with the angels; I'd read the last page. For vespers we wear the red-and-white-checked uniforms and our blue berets, and we use the Latin hymn book. You can recognize your uniform by the laundry number. Mine is 42; that way you can't make a mistake. Next to the number on our cotton undershirts is a label with a black woman on it.

Although I already know them by heart, I follow the words to "*Ave Maris Stella dei mater alma . . .*" my finger in the hymn part of the prayer book. You have to concentrate on following the words, that's what our catechism commands us to do. The saints are always very fervent and sincere when they pray. God does not accept your words when your mind is wandering. I fear Him. A hymn is not like other songs. It's a sweet and holy prayer. When you sing a hymn you go inside yourself. Even if you don't understand all the words you feel the music. When you say, "*Mater dei et Mater graciae*," you slow down and lower your voice because of the sad melody. Then I feel in my heart I would truly like to become a saint. "*O Maria, salve mater misericordiae . . .*" We poor sinners need God's mercy, His grace, and the help of Mary, His mother. She intervenes with her son because she is gentle and good. I see her high up over the altar, the Blessed Virgin, dressed in her long white veil, holding a crucifix and flowers, and the candles lit one by one, the tallest first. The sacred music is all around her and her son. The priest pulls the golden chains of the censer and little rings of smoke rise up toward the altar. It's special smoke. You breathe in the sacred odor in order to adore the divine; your soul sees the incense, the homage of the Three Kings, rise. It's solemn. God is the King of Kings. From His throne He triumphs over the whole world. I fear Him. It's already dark outside; the light is growing brighter in the chapel; it flickers and twinkles between the flowers on the altar. The sacred organ music, the voices of the faithful, and the incense all rise together far away to heaven. The white coifs on the sisters kneeling on the prie-dieus are like wings; they bend gently with the praying voices over our blue berets and our clasped hands.

For supper, they give us carrots cut up into little pieces. I stir them around with my fork and think of Moses's burning bush. He took his shoes off only because he didn't have a censer and was afraid of the Lord. I don't like cooked carrots. I hum *"Mater Dei . . ."* to myself. I hear Germaine and Claudine whispering and telling stories. I don't listen because of the incense and the angels with their hands clasped together. Sister Marie raps the table and calls for silence. The corners of the refectory are very dark and a big round lamp is lit next to the Blessed Virgin. I see the shadows of heads and my curls on the wall. Mademoiselle Laure is making me hurry with my food; I'm a slow eater. The chants we sang at vespers keep echoing in my head until after supper, when we move the benches back to make room for a ring dance. We form a circle, with Janine dancing in the middle and the rest of us singing and clapping our hands. "I choose the most beautiful of you to dance with me . . ." The same girls are always chosen. I stare at Germaine, who's dancing alone now. She's choosing. But she doesn't see me. I'm singing in a soft voice with no enthusiasm. I would like to be beautiful and dance in the middle and have it be my turn to choose. Mademoiselle Laure blows the whistle; it's bedtime.

After I've folded my bedspread and my smooth clean clothes, and put my two socks into my shoes, with the toes side by side, I choose the most beautiful holy picture in my bedside table. It's the Infant Jesus with long blond hair, a white robe, and sandals. He's holding a curly little lamb in His arms. I kneel before Him—my eyes are shut so that I won't be distracted, for His image is engraved on my heart—and I say, "Gentle Jesus, I love you, little Jesus, I adore you!" One shouldn't repeat the same words. "Son of Mary, Son of God. You suffer little children to come unto you. Your paradise is open only to them. See, I'm a little Christian girl now."

During our walk in the park today, Sister Anne taught us the parable of the little children. It's very important, because it's told by the disciple St. Matthew, who heard it preached by our Lord Jesus Christ. Our group is walking as usual, with Sister Marie in the middle. I stay behind them to listen and watch them walk. Sometimes I go up to the front to hear better. But they push me—I don't move fast enough and I'm always in somebody's way. Then, St. Matthew said, "Little children were brought to Him then that He might lay His hands on them and pray." "You see," Sister Marie explained, "He was blessing them. But the disciples rebuked them and Jesus said to them, 'Let the little children be . . . for of such is the kingdom of heaven.'"

We had caught some butterflies near St. Joseph's oratory, where we often go to pick flowers. They're sensitive to cold and like to sun themselves on rocks. This time, we also find some poppies and we sing, "Pretty poppies, my ladies, pretty little poppies." Rachel has caught a pretty yellow butterfly and crushed it between her hands. The wings have stuck to her fingers and she's shaking them because they're sticky. Sister Marie saw it and called her "cruel." But Rachel said that she hadn't done it on purpose. All the same, she laughed. She always laughs when she shouldn't. She's silly and so awkward! Her socks are always twisted and her smock is rumpled. She has very black, tangled, curly hair and her skin is sallow, not white like ours. The other day she knocked Alice over as she was jumping from a bench with her feet together. Sister Marie shouted, "You little idiot!" She turned red with fury. Everyone says Rachel's a nuisance. She never notices when she's annoying someone and she has that stupid laugh. She stands out like a sore thumb among the faithful in chapel. She arrived at the château a few days before my train, all alone. Nobody speaks to her. She isn't even baptized. She has neither eyes nor ears because she doesn't listen . . . she's a Jew. They say her family wants her back because things aren't going well with them. I wish she'd leave. She's like Mary Magdalene, the great sinner whom Jesus loved anyway, with her long black hair. Maybe her hair will grow when she's big and has grace and she'll wash the Lord's feet and dry them with her long hair. And then she'll anoint them with a precious, sweet-smelling balsam.

Saturday, the last time we took a shower, the elastic on her panties broke and she was squeezing her thighs together and wriggling and twisting, trying to keep them up. She was laughing and we were ashamed for her and we turned our heads away so that we wouldn't see her shameful parts. The soap had slipped from her hands into the dirty water. Her hair, wet under the shower, was trickling black on her face. Sister Anne grabbed her by the hand and shoved her into one of the senior girls' shower stalls, behind the curtains.

We take a shower every Saturday in order to be worthy of the Lord at High Mass on Sunday, the holy day. We cleanse our souls and our bodies. *I* don't take communion because I haven't been baptized yet; I can't receive Jesus in my heart. I can't confess, for the same reason, and my sins stay in my soul. Everything depends on baptism—it's the most important of the sacraments if you want to become a daughter of the Church. Also, they're waiting for my mother's answer. She may have left. We each have a stall in the shower room. The seniors have curtains on theirs because they have something else on their bodies and it's forbidden to look because of bad thoughts. The junior and intermediate students take everything off except their panties. Sister Anne watches over us; she says, "Wash yourselves well inside."

Inside, I know, is in your panties. It's not proper to say so because of the stains you get on your soul. I cover my hand with the soapy washcloth and pull back the elastic, not too much, without looking or thinking. I don't want to touch. It reminds me of Lorris when I was a heathen and knew Robert, the stationmaster's son.

My mother and I had gone away and were staying in a little house on the highway facing the fields, with a gentleman from the war of 1914. The house belonged to him; sometimes I'd go with him to help him weed his garden. He would take his cane, and I had a stick, too, which I leaned on as I limped beside him. He used to talk to himself out loud, saying that he was fed up, that they should leave him alone. My mother would pay him rent. There was a big black stove and we used to eat at the table, sitting next to him, but not too close. He used to eat some kind of pork—sticky tube-shaped things with flecks of blood—and drink wine. It smelled good. My mother said it was filthy. He wanted to give me some but he was afraid of her. Every evening he'd bring a newspaper home and read it for a long time. The war, he used to say, was getting on his nerves. Afterward, he would open the door of the grandfather clock to move the hand because, he would say, it was slow. I'd run my finger under the big newspaper letters to read and talk to myself.

Our house was very close to the station. When the train arrived, Robert, the stationmaster's son, would lower the barrier, the signal would clang, and the cars and wagons would wait. He was a big boy, thirteen years old. Sometimes he would take me on the bar of his bicycle. He would pedal very fast. But he didn't want to lend it to me. I'd rather have ridden it by myself.

Once, when I was watching Robert lower the barrier, he beckoned me and asked if I wanted a doll. How did he know that I liked dolls? He pulled me by the hand along the path by the rails. His house and even the houses in the village were already out of sight; all you could see was underbrush. He didn't have a doll in his hands and his pockets were flat. His hobnailed shoes were striking the stones. I was also wearing shoes with wooden soles. They gave them to us at City Hall, along with our tickets. We were walking close to the rails. I'm afraid of trains when they go by, making a terrible noise. I wanted to go home, but he said, "Wait a little, you'll see, didn't you say you liked dolls?" We came to a meadow with trees all around. "There, sit down over here," he said. "I don't want to get my pants dirty" was all I answered. "Don't worry, we'll take them off and I'm going to make you a pretty doll!" I no longer believed in his doll; we were far away, and I cried out that I wanted to leave. But he said in a mean voice, "Do what I tell you!" And he took off my pants. I was afraid and shut my eyes. Robert was doing something; I heard him undressing, he was touching me with his hand and putting something soft and warm . . . I didn't open my eyes; they were glued shut, even though I didn't know what Robert wanted me to touch. We were hidden far away. I was afraid to scream. What if someone was to come and see us like that, lying together in the grass! I held my hands tightly squeezed in front of me and Robert couldn't separate them. I wanted it to stop. Maybe now, I thought to myself, he'll let me ride the bicycle by myself. After Robert got up he didn't say anything more about the doll. He combed his hair back with his hands and we set out again along the same path. Only Robert walked very fast and didn't take my hand. I ran behind him. I was also afraid a train might arrive.

I never told my mother or anyone else about it. But now that I'm a Christian I have to drive away all bad thoughts and ask the Good Lord's forgiveness so that I can be sanctified and my heart remain pure. But I got his bicycle anyway, because of my friend, the German soldier.

One day, while my mother was feeding me lunch outdoors, some soldiers came from the station, running along the road. They were pushing a bicycle and arguing over it. It was my friend who was holding it; he would give it to me if I finished my soup. My mother didn't say anything. She never argues with anyone. I ate fast. Soon I was pedaling, but the bicycle wouldn't stop, it just rolled faster. I bumped against the sidewalk and fell. It didn't matter; I had a bike. I rode fast, leaving the trees and houses behind. It was so much better than walking. But I was afraid and suspected something was wrong: it was Robert's bicycle. Once, the bicycle turned all by itself toward the station. I fell onto the rails. The stationmaster came running to help me up. I shouted that I was all right and didn't let myself cry when he took my bike away. "Well now, where did you get this bicycle?" he asked. "My mother bought it for me!" He carried me under his arm like a package. I wiped my bloody knee on his jacket. He said, "It takes a brave little girl to ride such a big bicycle!" I answered, "It's mine." But my mother told him about the soldier's present. She apologized a lot and Robert's father took the bicycle away.

For a long time I walked with two bandages on my knees. Even without a bicycle I'm always falling down. The doctor says I have weak legs.

At the château now, we're doing pretty embroidery. One can make tapestries like a duchess. The seniors darn socks. Sitting on the benches across from the Sacred Heart, we embroider little crosses with colored yarn. Only I'm lazy and use long strands because it's annoying always to be threading the needle. I have no patience. Sister Marie says that I'm careless. We're all leaning over our canvases, pushing our needles with our thimbles. Sister Marie reads to us. Sometimes she reads the lives of the saints and martyrs, because we have to follow their example. She sits in the middle, her coif straight and her robe falling in even folds at her feet. She reads in a solemn voice. Today we listen to *The Orphan*. They say it's so sad it makes you cry. But it's nice. I love to listen. I can picture the people in the story: Vitalis and the little boy with the big head. I get a headache when I think of him. What a pity, the child hasn't long to live! The canvas falls on my knees. It doesn't matter. I'm no good at embroidery. Sister Marie says, "Mademoiselle, you're being careless and you're wasting yarn!" It hurts my eyes when I embroider a long time and I ruin my stitch. Sister Marie shows Claudine's work to everybody, praising it and holding it up as an example. All of a sudden we hear thunder— God's thunder! It's his anger. Some black clouds turn into rain by the château. Big drops are falling. Everyone shouts, "It's pouring! It's pouring!" And we take our work and run into the courtyard. Story hour is over. The girls are laughing because they got wet and it's funny to be taken by surprise like that. Sister Marie's coif is all limp. She holds it together in the middle with a pin that joins the two wings. Everyone's giggling and pretending not to notice. We don't know if she has any hair. I'd like her to go on with the story. I have no books of my own.

They say you can borrow books from the infirmary. You can read a lot of stories there and play cards. The infirmary is next to the chapel. You enter it by the same big staircase the sisters use to go to their rooms. Because they don't share our daily bread with us. They despise worldly goods, just as it is written. Even candy —I offered Sister Marie a piece of candy from my package and she refused. I've never seen her eat, or the other sisters, either. They abstain for the next world. And Sister Marie more than the others—she's a saint—you can see it by her paleness. The old students say that you can also get special treatment at the infirmary. Perhaps with the grace of God I'll get sick soon. If you have a temperature they call the village doctor. There's a sister on night duty who sleeps behind the screen. We laugh when one of the old-timers tells the story. She says that sometimes you can see her in her nightgown; at this point we laugh very loudly with our hands over our mouths—it's more polite. We ask ourselves if the doctor puts his ear over their hearts and touches them undressed when they're sick.

The doctor examines us every two weeks in our slips and socks in the office off the parlor. We all wait in line on the green carpet for our turn to be weighed. Our Mother Superior, Sister Cécile, opens our files on the desk in front of the doctor. Her coif is always askew—there's a black rim around the edge: her hair. It doesn't look very pious. But she's very busy with the papers on the desk and arranging for food to be delivered. She also talks on the telephone, to get coal. She can't be pious with the affairs of this world. She's the only one with a last name that you pronounce aloud: Marie-Louise Cortin. The others belong to the Lord. It's indiscreet to want to know sacred things.

Here we are, waiting in line; Thérèse has on a pretty white petticoat with ruffles and lace flounces just above the garters that hold up her long black stockings. Several of the girls are wearing whale-boned corsets. My mother wouldn't buy me one. Ginette is tugging at the medal of the Blessed Virgin on her chin and putting the little crucifix in her mouth. They all do that while they wait, chatting about their families and personal affairs. I don't say anything. My life is different and nobody knows about it. I like to listen and also watch how they weigh them on the scale. My turn comes. Mother Superior gets my papers ready on the desk. They are not Christian papers. She beckons and I get on the scale. My petticoat doesn't float in rippling waves of cloth like those of the other girls; it's made from a coarse sheet. My mother had made three of them, all alike, without lace or flounces.

Mother Cécile moves the metal cylinder across the bar with the numbers; I don't understand how she does it, but she says, "Twenty-one and a half kilos," and I know that I'm the lightest. I'm also puny and short. I decide to pay attention, from this day on, not to eat much, even when I'm hungry. "Doctor," says Mother Superior as she spreads my papers in front of him—they read my history. I'm not like the others. They keep me longer. The doctor tells me to lift my slip and puts his head against me. I know that he's listening to my heart.

Mother Superior comments that in order to build me up I will have to be given extra rations. I need good food. Some of the others have shadows on their lungs and you can hear a tearing noise when they cough. Because, like me, many of them came here for their health through the Red Cross. Josette always ends up with a coughing spell when she talks or laughs. She has a loose, phlegmy cough; it's very important if you want to be sent to the infirmary. Her face becomes red and she chokes. Her lungs are affected.

I look out the window at the park fence beside the chapel. It's the prettiest of the venerable places. The trees there are tall and straight, the gravel well raked. It's a good place to meditate. Boxwood hedges and thickets border the château. Hedges and palm branches are the favorites of the Good Lord and, of course, of the dead; they're sacred.

The yellow circles on the ceiling swing under the night light; several of them have haloes and, between the cracks, little black specks. I pull my knees up because the sheets are too long and cold. I'll stretch them out later, but not right away. A shadow flits on bare feet and makes the floor creak near the big toilet pail. Someone lifts the lid and I hear her putting it on the floor. Then there's the sound of pee hitting the pail. You're not supposed to listen but I can't help myself. *I* can do it without making a noise, you have to practice. It's Martine. She's part of the group that's going to be baptized the day after tomorrow. Her mother has given her consent. She runs to her bed on tiptoe. I can hear the mattress creak. *I* get into bed carefully, so as not to disturb the sheets. I like to be all neatly tucked in under the covers, with my nightgown pulled over my legs without a wrinkle. Then I can talk to Jesus and Mary—it's proper. Thérèse snores, then begins again with little whistles like a refrain; she doesn't even know it. It's strange at night with all the shadows when I can't sleep. It's like a dream, and my mind wanders nonsensically. But actually I can think about the things that happen during the day. Except that, when I look up at the yellow ceiling and the night light, I fall asleep in the middle of it all, and in the morning it's not the same.

. . . The yellow ceiling . . . the desert . . . the desert of Judea. "Now in those days John the Baptist came, preaching in the desert of Judea . . ." He's the one who invented baptism with the water of the Jordan. He called for all the sinners to come and he said to them, "I indeed baptize you with water, for repentance; Repent, for the kingdom of heaven is at hand."

At catechism, they teach us about baptism because some of us didn't receive the sacrament at birth due to the ignorance of our parents. There are eighteen of us souls in the dark. The priest wrote to our parents a long time ago so that the kingdom of heaven would be open to us in case we were suddenly to die. But we're not completely lost. There's a place that's not so bad— Limbo.

The trouble is, you can't see God's light there. All the saints are there with the Blessed Virgin. Really though, it's not worth it without God or His Son. In the meantime, our souls are still stained with Original Sin because of the man who ate the forbidden fruit. The important thing is to have a place in heaven after death.

The Church receives its children for baptism and then gives them a certificate with a baptismal name—the name of a great saint, a patron who protects them against temptations and accidents. Through the grace he has, being near to God, he also helps them in many ways.

I'm still waiting for my mother's answer. She promised in her last letter to send me a package with the things I'd asked for. But she didn't say anything about my baptism.

We've learned a nice hymn. It's now my favorite because of the sacred music about the Blessed Virgin and the words; it's made especially for me. "Thou the Immaculate . . . abandon us not . . ." She is certainly very good in this song. Perhaps she will be able to help me. Everyone is stained except her and her son, of course, and everyone in their family. It's not certain about Joseph, even though he's part of the Holy Family. For us mortals born of woman, it's better to be baptized with the water of the Jordan—the true water, the water of the Lord.

Almost everyone has now received permission. They inform them in the parlor and prepare them for their day of joy. I'm the only one left. Always the last, and even then it's not certain. My mother can play tricks on me when it comes to things like that. It's like the betrayal by the disciples in the Gospel. She doesn't understand how important the word of God is. Because you can be damned. Maybe it's a sign that my mother is no longer in Paris. O God, please perform a miracle! Tomorrow is the big day; it's also Corpus Christi.

Sister Marie has summoned me to the parlor. It's very serious. She says, "My child," in a sad voice that I've never heard before. Her eyes, behind the desk, meet mine with a kind, special look. I lower my head. It is difficult to look at the light in the faces of those who are close to God. My mother must have said no. Somewhere, deep down, I think sister is trying to cajole me into something. She repeats, "My child, your mamma does not accept the precepts of our religion. You must submit to the authority of your mother." But I understand, it's a lost cause. I'm not going to be one of the elect. I remain silent. Nevertheless, I am thinking very hard that it is not my mother's business—it's *my* soul. But she is no longer my mother: I want to be a daughter of the Church.

Sister Marie stands up, her habit rustling; I follow her to the sacristy. In the mirror, you can see the big crucifix, the statues, and me with them, all at the same time. I know myself now. I have blue eyes—that's the color of purity—and blond curls like Jesus. I have pretty hair—that's vanity. I make a face, the way I used to in Paris, in front of the mirror. Christ must have seen. Sister Marie is opening a secret drawer. She gives me a brand-new medal and a silver chain. "Take it, my child, it will protect you. Pray, be obedient, and God will grant you His grace. Be humble and charitable toward your companions." These are beautiful words like those in the prayers and I stop thinking how angry I am at my mother. But she hasn't told me whether I'm still going to Limbo—it's the rule.

During lunch I wear the medal over my smock. But it's not to show off—I pray to the Blessed Virgin. It touched the cabbage in my bowl while I was eating, and I dried it with my napkin. They say it doesn't count when it's silver. It's more precious when it's gold. They have thousands of medals of saints and patrons—they hide them in their uniforms so as not to show pride. I didn't tell them about my mother's letter and the baptism. I'm ashamed. Perhaps God will perform a miracle, but He won't have time—it's for tomorrow. And then, if through a miracle He should take away my Original Sin, how will everyone know?

During our walk around the park, Sister Anne teaches us the virtue of repentance when you sin after baptism. We learn the sins by heart: pride, that's the mother of all vices. The newborn who die after baptism are lucky, they go directly to heaven. The others, who continue to live by the grace of God, are troubled by endless temptations, but confession—the second sacrament—absolves them. That way, you don't have time to die without forgiveness. The Lord is indulgent, so you can keep your soul white for communion when you receive Him in your heart.

During vespers, I pray very hard that God will hear my prayer—just mine; it's very important for tomorrow. I kiss my medal with devotion: Please, I need a miracle! During hymns, I almost send the music off pitch. I want God to hear my voice over all the others, for Him to grant my prayer; it's urgent—for tomorrow—because I'm denied the most important grace of all on account of my origins. I'm wearing the wrong beret. The one I took is too big. It fell off during benediction, in the part where you bow your head. Rachel laughed out loud—the blasphemous girl!

Today's the big day. We hurry to get ready for the procession and the joyous feast. We don't do everyday things anymore. They've prepared outfits all in white, the sign of purity, for the girls who are going to be baptized in the village church. The rest of us wear blue uniforms with white checks, and white hats for Corpus Christi. We file out toward the entrance gate of the park, where we wait in two separate lines, holding our rosaries and prayer books. The villagers are standing in clusters at the crossroads and in the street. The church bells are ringing joyously: our schoolmates are being baptized. The bells resound over the whole countryside, announcing the great event. Now we see them arrive, a white cloud floating at the head of the processional altar. One by one the newly baptized approach, their white crowns interwoven with roses. The villagers all look at them. They have become true Christians. We start singing, "I am Christian . . ." I sing softly; my windpipe hurts and I feel a tugging at my throat . . . The bells drown out our song; they say, "Baptism, baptism," and doves fly up among them as happened long ago at the baptism of Christ: "The heavens were opened to him and he saw the Spirit of God descending as a dove and coming upon him." They arrive at our Avenue, the girls in white, gold missals between their white gloves and mother-of-pearl rosaries on their wrists. We are going to congratulate them in the sacristy; a special message from the Pope has come from Rome. The procession passes in front of us, the altar protected under a large, square, gilded and fringed umbrella. The choir children, dressed in lace, are holding the big cross. But the church bells drown out everything else and our ears are filled with baptism.

The sun is shining; my hands are damp and leave a finger pattern on the book cover. Sister Marie's coif is as transparent as paper and she's blinking. Thérèse raises her hand to shield her face from the sun. She's wearing a pretty ring with a small heart. *I* know how to make rings out of strings and beads. Once I made a ring for each of my fingers. *That* was rich. My mother used to have a pretty ring that blazed and flashed fire. I would put it on my thumb. But she sold it before we left, to get papers. It's very important for us to get papers and it's expensive.

The refectory is ready for the feast. The long tables have been pushed against the wall and a special table has been set in the middle before the Blessed Virgin, in honor of the girls just baptized. It is covered with garlands of flowers. I can't see it all from my seat. But then, it's no longer mine, we've changed places. We also have clean napkins with different napkin cases, folded like pockets. On the side, each of us has a cream puff; that's the dessert for feast days. Jacqueline arrives first, a big white bow in her hair. She loves to dress up. That's vanity for a Christian. And capricious—anytime she cries for her mother you have to give in to her. During grace I stand on tiptoe to get a better view of the things on their table; cones filled with sugar-coated almonds, red wine in glasses: that's the Lord's blood, which the priest drinks from a chalice during Mass. They eat from real, white plates. We've been given the same old tin.

Today, we're allowed to talk. But we're not noisy. It's serious and we concentrate on our food—it's very good; it's roast beef. The juice oozes out and makes puddles on the plate, but the mashed potatoes mop it up. Mademoiselle Laure says, "Be careful not to stain your clothes!" The girls who've been baptized get double portions of melon. Thérèse says again that she loves cream puffs. I ask her for her piece of melon in exchange for my cream puff. I now have two, like the girls in the middle of the room, the ones who've been baptized. Jacqueline hands out sugar-coated almonds from a large cone. I put them in my pocket to look at later. Rachel has taken a great many, she cheats with both hands. We get up from table, our bellies stuffed with baptismal treats.

Everyone has gone, I don't know where. Today, we can do as we please. We can even go to the toilet without raising our hands to ask permission. I'm sitting alone on the steps under the arcade. I'm not doing anything. I'm not even thinking about anything, I just look at the Sacred Heart on the lawn. I've put my smock back on so as not to get dirty and I touch the almonds in my pocket. Yet deep down, I feel that I have failed. Something is troubling me and I feel confused, but it's no use dwelling on it with a full stomach. I hiccup, then throw up. The second piece of melon comes up, the one they got for being baptized. It's bitter; perhaps it's like the gall that Jesus drank on the cross. My stomach feels heavy and my legs are twined around each other like a wreath. I've seen Thérèse like that when she's doing needlework. There now is a really correct position. A drop falls on my arm; I think to myself that maybe it's the Lord causing water to fall on me; I wait for the miracle. Only there's no rain in the sky, it's all blue. It's bird droppings, white with green and black streaks. I look up and see a nest in the gutter. Something moves, a twig falls. I pick it up and draw lines on the ground. I don't know how to draw. The baptismal bells are still ringing in my head. I look in my pocket for a pink-coated almond. I crunch it, taking care not to crack the almond. Almonds grow in Palestine, too. It's the disciples' favorite food, that and wild honey. Like John the Baptist. He also ate locusts. I swallow the remains of the sugar. You can divide an almond in half by the little cleft down the middle. I spit it out. Saliva is like gossamer, it's disgusting. But nobody's here. When you're all alone you can do what you want. "But don't you know that Jesus sees everything?" I don't think that those things interest Him. Good manners are not His concern. I throw the almond onto the ground. I'm not going to eat it and I crush it underfoot between the pebbles. "For thee, oh Lord, I will deprive myself." I hear the whistle. It's time for tea.

Paulette has been called to the parlor. People are whispering that it's bad news. Her mother's been sick for a long time. We've been praying for her. Everybody knows that she's an unhappy little girl; her father is dead. She has to keep her mouth open all the time because her teeth stick out—just two of them with a gap between—over her open lips. It runs in the family. Sister Anne is there now, in front of the chapel, holding Paulette's hand. She cries and everybody runs to her. She's an orphan. They caress her and cry with her. "Don't cry, Paulette!" they say. Some of them go to their lockers to fetch presents for her. They wipe her nose, dry her eyes, and kiss her a lot. I watch it all from a distance, I don't go near. I'm unable to console anyone. I'm afraid of orphans. I still like sad songs about very sick people, though. When her mother was sick, we used to sing a pretty hospital song: "It is Sunday today, Mamma darling, here are some white roses, for you who love them so . . ."

Monique, big Monique, our leader, kisses and strokes Paulette. She even keeps the others away. She's so sweet and gentle. You have to see how rough she can be in games. She'll stop at nothing to win. She's very strong but, as Sister Marie says, too bossy. We're all in dread of her.

We often play ball at game time. The other day we lost because of me. Monique had taken me on her team because I was the only one left. Before each game, the captains choose sides—the most daring are chosen first. We're all there waiting. Ever since we've been playing war like this—real war with prisoners—we know who's strongest and can make their team win. They already know about me. I love to play but I'm afraid. I'm really a coward. What a lot of courage it takes to catch the ball and win for your team! Anyhow, Monique was our captain and was giving the orders. While her teammates get into position she holds the heavy ball up high, deftly aiming it straight at the enemy. We shout, "Got you! Prisoner!" She mows them all down. It's fantastic! And I, I run all over the place as the ball whips by, flailing about. But there, even Monique the great has been caught! Now we know it's a lost cause, but we try to free her; we do everything we can in our struggle not to lose. The enemy spares me, they'll get me later. It's easy. Dear God, help me save my team, I whisper. But I know that one mustn't call on God for this kind of thing. The prisoners on my team are all pinning their hopes on me. I really wanted so much to show my courage. I dart in and out as they come at me. I run. The ball brushes against me. I'm hot and I have a stitch in my side. The prisoners on my team shout, "Go on, catch it, don't be afraid!" Suddenly a violent blow straight in my face throws me to the ground. I've dropped the ball. The prisoners all cry, "What a drip!"

During supper, as I'm peeling my potato in my bowl, I think of the heavy ball; I'm holding it. That night, after praying to the holy pictures, I become the captain of the team. With one hand I'm holding the huge ball, and then, one by one, I take them all prisoner. My side cries, "Hurrah for our captain!" That's me! But I look up at the ceiling. I know I'll never make it.

A new trainload of girls has arrived from Dunkirk and Lille. We call them daughters of the North. Seniors. There are a great many of us now: a hundred and fifty at the château de Beaujeu.

The new girls learn all the rules of conduct. We're held up as examples to them. They tell us stories of things that have happened. I know a lot now, and I'm first in catechism among the juniors.

Christiane, a girl from Dunkirk, has been placed across from me at table, under the Marshal's photo. When she eats she pushes her fork with her bread and she curls her little finger like a marquise. She's as pretty as a saint with her long curly hair and big brown tearful eyes. But she doesn't cry. It's not her nature. She has asthma like St. Bernadette. It seems she has attacks and can't breathe. She's fifteen. I like her a lot. She also has a brown spot under one eye—it's a beauty spot.

When we're eating, I look at her and she smiles back. She seems to be talking to me. But she doesn't say anything, except that sometimes she just calls, laughingly. She's become team captain, too, and she hasn't any calves. Her legs are very thin. But she knows how to give orders and people obey her.

They tell us a lot of stories now—a fire at Dunkirk, where there were English soldiers and time bombs. Christiane says she barely escaped; the boats were sinking in the sea, her brother was on one of them. The people of Dunkirk are very proud.

Christiane has arranged a Punch and Judy show for the evening. God, but she's plucky! Sister Marie lets her do anything. She has set up the soup-pot table in front of the refectory door that goes to the kitchen and has dressed herself up as a perfect Punch, in a long coat. It seems somebody else was working the hands. It was a lot of fun and we laughed a lot, the same as at the Tuileries gardens. Afterward, we all sang together, in separate groups, to see which would be louder. I shouted with the Parisians, "Long live Paris, wonderful town, with all our loves we'll settle down; long live Paris, long live Paris!" But victory went to the daughters of Dunkirk. They were shouting, "Jean Bart, Jean Bart!"—a pirate. It's very important to win for your hometown. Now, each city is at war. I'm on the Parisians' side.

I sit with Thérèse, the pious, at tea; she's finishing my piece of chocolate. I draw some circles with a stick: the moon. I've dug up a sticky earthworm. I pick it up with the stick and say to Thérèse, "See, you can cut it in half and it will go on living." I twist the worm's moist pink ends. Yvonne, the Parisian, sings, "She was reading *le p'tit Parisien*, she was interested in poli . . . tics."

And afterward, you can cut it up in pieces. I already have four and the little ends are wriggling. I turn them over with my stick and sing, "Poli . . . tics . . . poli . . . tics."

They said a special Mass for the soul of Paulette's mamma. It's beginning to get cold. The juniors move from the château to the pink pavilion: a little house, past the linden trees and pigpens, from which you can see the tower of the four Germans. At night we go to the pink pavilion helped by a flashlight that Mademoiselle Laure holds; it's scary between the big trees. I think of Tom Thumb in the forest and run between the other girls so as not to be alone on the path should a ghost appear.

The pink pavilion is small and warm. We take our naps in the big room in the attic. Naps are very boring. The walls have cracks and you can make drawings with your eyes while you're lying down. I've discovered that when you keep your eyes open a long time they smart and tears come without your feeling sad. When I want to cry I know how and someone will come to comfort me. Maybe I'll cry like that in the dormitory this evening and Sister Marie will come and tuck me in. I want so much for her to see me sad and devout. She'll also see that I'm holding the wooden crucifix she gave me to pray with over my heart. Nowadays I'm very devout. Only I don't dare. They aren't real tears.

After our nap, Thérèse wants to comb my pretty hair. I say, "You want some of it, I'll give you some!" I grab a lock, pull it out by the roots, and look at it in my outstretched hand. She jumps back with a nervous laugh, her hands behind her back, and starts to run. Josette is coughing. She always has bronchitis. I ask Josette if *she* wants some of my hair. I pull out another lock, it hurts. She recoils. I say, "Take it, it's mine, I'm giving it to you!" To myself I say, "Look, it's beautiful, I want you to have it with all my heart!" I like to give presents, it gives me pleasure. She takes the hair and runs away. I feel funny. I see my lock of hair in the distance, falling onto the cement. A gust of wind carries it away, scattering it along the Avenue.

I received the package with the little scissors. They have lavender handles made of bone. They're very pretty and I keep them in my locker so as not to damage them. That same day we'd been out on the lawn picking some tall plants. Sister Anne is teaching us how to weave baskets with rushes. We make real little baskets. If I were in Paris I'd go to the market with them. Baskets are very useful. Paulette asks me for my scissors to cut the rushes with; I've left them in my locker. And I don't know why, I'm thinking that it's the last package I'll get from my mother. I don't get letters from her anymore. Paulette asks me again with her pleading orphan's eyes. I can't refuse because of the compassion one owes one's neighbor. I'm afraid for my scissors, but I give them to her. My heart sinks thinking about my mother working in the market. Paulette brings them back almost instantly: one of the handles has broken. God, I knew it! "They can be fixed," she says sweetly. She smiles with her two teeth sticking out. She's afraid of me. I don't answer. You can't say anything to an orphan. But inside I feel such a desire to cry and to hit her, I'm choking with rage. My scissors! My mother's scissors are broken. Paulette did not offer to fix them. Sister Anne tried, she's very clever with her hands. She gave them back to me glued. Even in chapel, I can't stop thinking about my scissors.

The sun has gone from the lawn around the Sacred Heart. It's raining hard and thundering. Last night a man from Beaujeu was struck by lightning near a tree. We were very frightened. I recited the creed three times in bed. But the thunder was so loud, with the lightning, that the noise stopped me from praying. I was calling to God, the almighty. Little Jesus is too small, He can't stop loud noises at night.

Going around the park, we walk slowly in the mud, dragging our feet through the wet leaves, because of the church bells tolling for the man struck by lightning. They are going to bury him in the church at Beaujeu. Madeleine, who is walking arm in arm with Sister Marie, says that you must never stand under trees—they attract lightning. But the château has lightning rods, way up in the sky, that protect us. You can see, behind them, the big tower of Beaujeu, where the four Germans are staying. At night their searchlights cast circles of light on our park: they guard the territory. Madeleine also says—she's an expert on storms—that you shouldn't wear metal objects, they attract lightning. We collect the fallen leaves on the Avenue and pick them between the veins to make spiders. Then we sneak off to tickle the necks of some of our unsuspecting friends, the silly fools!

When it rains we stay inside the courtyard; after catechism, we can do as we please. Adèle has brought some marbles and I watch her and her friends playing, squatting on the cement. She aims and says, "Bing!

Bang! Hit!" The marbles knock against each other and roll away, green and yellow. They look like eyes. It's a boys' game. Of course, you have to be able to aim like a street kid, with one eye half closed and munching your lip. "Bang!" And she sings, "Eeny, meeny, miney mo, catch an Arab by the toe . . ." What a braggart! The rest of us sing the refrain: "Muhammad, the great prophet . . . Allah, Allah . . ." She says there are lots of Arabs in Algeria—she's from there. They pray to Muhammad lying in the sand. She's seen a great many caravans on their way from the Sahara, the vast desert . . . "Bang! . . . hit!"

Here comes Henriette! They stop their games abruptly and move back to watch her pass; we're all in awe of her. But she goes by in silence, without seeming to notice us. We don't dare speak to her. She's tall and thin; she's fifteen. We follow her with our eyes, not making a sound, as she goes to her locker. She looks as though she's floating through the air. The inner part of one of her shoes is torn, but that doesn't matter to her. She takes out a book; no one knows what she has in her locker. And we don't dare try to trick her into letting us get a look because she's who she is—Henriette. No one ever bothers her the way they do the others. Sometimes some of the seniors gather around and tell her their secrets. But she doesn't say anything to them, except when she's asked something; she listens. The sisters never scold her. She's not like the others. I watch her from a distance and would like to get closer to her. She's Jewish.

Adèle starts rolling marbles again. "Hit!" She wins. Martine stands up, shouting, "You're cheating!" and punches her on the ear. Before you know it, they're attacking each other with hands and teeth, tangled together, kicking and slapping each other. The rest of us move away. They're fighting hard. I think to myself that one should separate them and help one's neighbor in the quarrel, like Jesus. But that's the way it is in rough fighting—there's nothing you can do really, even when you're Christian. Besides, they don't like you to interfere. Sister Anne gets there too late. Martine has a bloody nose, poor thing, and that horrible Adèle's smock is torn; she touches the sore spot on her cheek and collects her marbles, muttering something to let us know that she's going to get her revenge. She's very vindictive, you have to watch out for her. I want to go up and tell her that it's forbidden. Our Lord Jesus gave us an example of goodness. I feel something welling up, getting bigger and bigger. I know, I have the call. I'd like to talk to her. But Adèle has a temper and she's strong, she's bent on vengeance. I see Henriette a little way off, reading on the bench. She's very intelligent, she's first in catechism in the senior class. I've never seen her either play ball games or jump rope. Sometimes in chapel I turn around to look—and I can't see her praying or singing. It's in her heart. Sister Marie, the strict one, gives her special attention. Henriette is not like the others. I'd like to speak to her but I don't dare. As soon as I approach her, my palms begin to sweat. I know that she hasn't been baptized, either.

Rachel has left. They say her parents have been taken away. Her uncle is claiming her. I knew it would end badly; her name alone is a bad omen, Diamond: it has the sound of dying in it. We're well rid of her. She was so stupid. But at the back of my mind something is bothering me and I can't pray the way I should.

There are only two of us left now at the château, I mean two Jews. Everyone knows, but nobody says anything. We're all fervent Christians. Oh, Henriette! I'm so happy to know you're there, even though you don't say anything to me.

Sunday is All Souls' Day and my birthday—I was born that day. It's my first birthday here. I feel sad, almost like crying. I don't know why. I don't want to grow up. They give me an extra pat of butter at breakfast for my birthday. I put it on a tiny crust of bread. It makes big yellow eyes and haloes in my coffee and melts in my mouth like black-market butter. It's very good, but it's all gone almost immediately. I think of the Mass for the dead. It's the Mass for all the dead and we sing a special hymn: *"De profundis clamavi ad te domine . . ."* All the songs for the dead are in Latin—that makes it sadder, gives you gooseflesh and puts the fear of God in you. You don't really sing—you recite softly, in cadences, like the droning at the cemetery. It makes you think of burials, tombs, and real death. The chapel is dark. The dead don't need light. First we pray for all the dead in our family. In my family no one dies. Then we pray for all the dead of the earth. Their souls descend to our little chapel to listen to our lamentations. Souls don't take up space. Their bodies are in the ground and don't move. Except for ghosts and phantoms, and the spirits that move tables and make people talk. I've seen pictures like that, dead people who lament in their graves until the Last Judgment because of their sins. Death is very scary. *I* am never going to die. I've never seen a dead person, except in Lorris with my mother.

In the main square, a German soldier had shot at an enemy plane and the plane returned the fire. I saw the soldier far off lying on the sidewalk. His black boots were stretched out and his body was covered by a green cape. The people all crossed over to the opposite sidewalk; he was lying flat without moving: that's how you saw he was dead. Going home, my mother wanted to pass by him. I was afraid and stood at a distance, looking at his boots, which didn't move. We passed right in front of him and I threw up. I cried because of the vomit and dead people. I felt ill afterward. When we got back to the square, the German wasn't there anymore.

But here it's not the same; we sing hymns for the dead about eternal life. You have to believe in the Last Judgment, when the dead rise from their graves, so really you're not dead at all.

It rains endlessly; the refectory windows are dripping with long streams of water. Perhaps this is the flood. The air is full of "*De profundis clamavi . . .*" and the souls of ghosts. I feel lazy watching the trees lifting their twisted limbs. I write my name on the pane with my finger. I can hear the wind. Thérèse knows a sleep-walker who goes to the cemetery at night and opens coffins. I saw some slugs while I was running to the courtyard. They dribble slime and they're all sticky when they move. Jacqueline crushed one and it stuck to the sole of her shoe all yellow. She was crying. We found it disgusting. At noon Christiane tells how a great lord made his enemies disappear in the dungeons of his castle. He was a hypocrite; he invited them, then had them lean against a chest. The wall opened and they fell into the dungeons and died there, without food.

They found their skeletons and a place on the wall where fingernails had scratched for help. They're really terrifying stories; they scare me so I can't even move. But I love to listen. We have dungeons, too, in our château, a whole wing closed off. It's haunted. When you pass by, near the stairs, you run because of the ghosts; some of them make noises to frighten me. I don't lean against walls anymore.

The Parisians dance the minuet, the dance of the kings and queens of France, two by two taking little steps and making graceful gestures like great ladies to the tune of "Would you care to dance, Marquise, will you dance the minuet . . . Tra la la la . . ." The marquis moves in a circle around the marquise. The minuet is the king's polka. It's a song as slow as rain; it makes you sleepy, and you yawn. There are no more kings in France. I go to look at the flies on the windowpane. The Parisians sing in chorus the song about the corpse in the amphitheater who was bored stiff with the other corpses.

In the Gauls' hut, on the way to the pink pavilion, they also have corpses of Vercingetorix's Gauls. It's a stone hut with a thatched roof. Martine says she saw some skulls inside. We all scream with terror. We never go near the hut in the evening. I like Vercingetorix very much. I've seen pictures of him in my schoolbook, in Paris. He was a fearless hero. At Clermont-Ferrand, he led his men with great firmness against his enemies. He beat the Romans in the first pages of the book. I used to leaf through the pictures and look at the brave Gauls surrounding their leader, until the page where he was taken prisoner by the Romans. I hate the Romans. And I would never turn the page where Vercingetorix is in chains. It made me feel very sad. They were pagans, the Gauls. They worshipped idols and mistletoe. But you really have to forgive them because they were our ancestors. And the French are their descendants, a valiant people. I am proud to be French. After we beat the Romans, the disciples converted them. And ever since then, God is the only Lord. I've converted, too. How lucky I am!

Jesus knows me now. I pray, my eyes shut and my hands joined with my fingers straight. I say my own prayers with words invented by me. I'm waiting for voices to give me a divine sign, but in the meantime, I can make up for not being baptized through good deeds, as in the lives of the saints. I really know my catechism —I'm first in the junior class. I'm always the first to answer. The last time I explained the parable of the unmerciful servant. His fellow servant had pleaded with him because of his debt, but he did not have his Lord's compassion and he strangled him, saying, "Pay what thou owest!" Sister Anne said, "Very good, my child!" I looked at the others, happy and proud. But I'm not conceited. Some people just don't understand, like Peter, who was always asking Jesus questions. That fellow's really the silliest of the disciples; what's more, he got frightened in the water when he began to sink. All the same, he was Jesus' favorite, after John, his well-beloved. I think Jesus loved the humble, people who were a little bit foolish; he had a lot of patience. But one really mustn't think like that when it comes to religion. Jesus said, Those who are poor in intelligence are blessed. It's not their fault. The important thing is to have faith. I am intelligent and I have faith. I know the names of the disciples by heart, even the names their families called them when they were atheists and fishermen. Only, I have one big fault. I speak before I'm called on, without raising my hand. Sister Anne says that I'm impatient. I'm afraid someone else will answer before I can. Each time, I promise myself I won't do it anymore. Germaine asked me to recite all the sacraments in order. We count them off on our fingers. Everyone is listening to me. I'm preaching. If only Henriette could see me now. Afterward, we repeat the parable of the lord of the vineyard. As soon as the catechism lesson's over, they forget everything and run out to skip rope. I play, too, but I think about the lesson. I can't help myself. If only I could speak to Henriette. Everyone knows that she's the first among the first—the best scholar in the senior class. She's the one you go to with difficult questions. But one doesn't always dare. How I'd love to be in the senior class with Henriette! The catechism they do is much more advanced.

From the courtyard windows, we watch the snow fall in little white petals. It melts right away; that's too bad. We're going to have real snow for Christmas. We stand in line to go to the bathrooms. There are three lines; Bernadette is in the intermediate line. She's leaning against the door of the sister in charge, looking sad as she listens to the others chatter. I tell her that she has a pretty name, the name of a revered saint. She shrugs her shoulders but doesn't respond. I know that she's worried about something. She's nice. She's thirteen years old and comes from the town of Troyes. Bernadette wears peasant clogs and her father does manual labor. She senses that I'm watching her and, with a sigh, brushes back a lock of hair from her forehead. Yesterday she finished knitting a little dress for her youngest sister. She wanted to go home to help her mamma. Her father doesn't want to work. I tell her that she must have faith in God; with God all things are possible. She looks at me with her big green eyes—like the green on the wings of big flies—and, screwing them up, says, "It's all very well for you to talk! I have five brothers and sisters; my mother's expecting again. It never ends!" "What never ends?" I ask. She starts to laugh. "You're so naïve!" and she adds, in a nicer tone, "There're too many of us at home and I'm the oldest." I have a wonderful idea: "You're very lucky that God sent your family so many children. If only He'd give me a brother or sister, how happy I'd be!" Bernadette grows sad again and lowers her head. "My father drinks. I have to go home to work and take care of the little ones." I'm amazed to hear her telling me all her family secrets so freely. She sees me as very young. I'm seven and a half. She hasn't got faith because of her family. I'm so happy to have found a straying soul. She will listen to me. I look Bernadette straight in the eyes; she's pure—she doesn't look away. Eyes are the windows of the soul. But it's hard to talk to her, she becomes silent. Maybe she'll listen to the Divine Word. I tell her that she must pray in her heart for God's help, beg him with special words to make her father work again. Talking, I feel hot, as though I had a fever. I go on. "His bounty is infinite, His power great . . ." She listens to me, making circles on the pavement with the toe of her clog. It gets on my nerves. At last, she raises her head and looks at me the way grownups look at children. Then I know that she's thinking of other things—things she's not going to tell me. I wonder what Henriette would have said. I've missed my turn to go to the toilet. But I don't feel like it anymore. Anyway, I didn't want to go to that place with God's name on my lips.

Now that we're sleeping in the pink pavilion—the junior and intermediate students—we can hear the pigs snoring at night in the outer courtyard. They're the ones they're fattening up for Christmas. This morning I didn't hear the wake-up call. Mademoiselle Laure pulled my covers back; my nightie was rolled up. I'm afraid the others saw everything. My cheeks are hot and the light hurts my eyes. The girls, their towels over their shoulders, are already in line for lice inspection. Sister Marie comes and feels my forehead. They bring a thermometer and some Vaseline. Ah, I'm happy! I have 102. I'm going to the infirmary! It's enough to keep me in bed a long time with books and cards. I have a headache. Mademoiselle Laure takes me, wrapped up in a blanket, to the château infirmary; we climb the big staircase with the waxed steps and gold banister. The infirmary is all white and has eight beds. I am alone. There're big windows and you can see the lawn from the balcony. Little pink clouds form a roof over the Sacred Heart. The Blessed Virgin looks beautiful in her blue dress with stars. Jesus is very little in her arms. It's Our Lady of the Rosary. I feel the cold sheets with my hot hands. My head is throbbing on the pillow. I'll have time to pray to the Blessed Virgin all day long. There are bouquets of purple flowers on Sister's screen —always the same pattern of flowers running the whole length of the screen; it's irritating. This evening I'll hear Sister getting undressed. At noon they bring me some broth in a real china dish on a tray. I eat the white bread they give sick people and use the inside to make a die with my fork, with six little holes so that I can win at dominoes.

Sister Anne brings me a book, *The Good Children.* You see pictures of them on every page. But I don't feel well and the words jump around on the page. The good children are very obedient. They do good deeds on every page. Even though it's a big book, I already know how it ends. At teatime Sister says I still have a high temperature and I drink some lime-flower tea with pieces of dried seeds swimming in it. The doctor is coming tomorrow. I feel drained. I'll finish the book another time, and I'll pray twice as much tomorrow. In the sky over the Sacred Heart the clouds drive a dragon with a puffing engine.

"We're bringing you company!" says Sister Marie as she opens the door. It's Christiane, wrapped in a long cape that reaches her feet. Her hair is all in disorder. They give her two pillows and put a little bottle on the bedside table. Sister says something in a low voice before she leaves. Christiane is lying in bed, her eyes closed. Her long curls are tucked under the sheet. She's holding a handkerchief to her nose and tears are running over her flounced sleeves, embroidered with forget-me-nots. She doesn't say a word; she doesn't even smile now, the way she did in the refectory under the Marshal. I'm curious, but I control myself and say nothing. I've learned to control myself since I've become a Christian. It's already dark outside. The night light casts haloes over the mound of pillows under her head. She must have some serious illness. Maybe she's going to die; no one has died yet at the château. If only Henriette were here. How I wish Henriette were ill, too. Maybe God will perform a miracle.

Sister Gabrielle has come in quietly and gone behind the screen. I listen—she's unlocking a closet. It sounds as though she's taking out her nightgown. I'm going to tell everyone about it. I hear the sound of material—it's her pulling up her robe; she takes it off. Then she sits on the bed—it creaks—because she's pulling her stockings off . . . If the girls at the château only knew! Sister Gabrielle is behind the screen without her habit, in her bed without her coif! I lift my head a little to see if Christiane is listening, too. She's sleeping. Why do I have bad thoughts? I hear Christiane breathing, loud and fast. It's funny, her blanket is raised. Maybe she's play-acting; she knows a lot of magic tricks and tricks with puppets. She's brave, like the patron of her home-town, Dunkirk. We Parisians learned the hymn to Jean Bart from her. Christiane has pictures of his statue in the main square in Dunkirk. She's tough. She must be from the same family as Jean Bart.

All of a sudden she screams, "I'm suffocating, I can't breathe!" lifting her arms toward the night light like a saint beseeching the heavens. She's making loud noises, her mouth open. Sister Gabrielle comes running in a white gown and a bonnet. It may be a slip, but I can't get a good look at her because of Christiane, who's going to die. Sister undoes the collar of her nightie and raises the pillow. Then she says, on the phone, "Christiane is having an asthma attack." She's lucky, like St. Berna-dette. She has fallen back, gasping, on the pillow; her hands are contorted. "I'm suffocating, give me air!" It's real suffering; it's too bad, it prevents her from offering it to God. I am afraid she's going to die. It must be terrible to be with no air like that—like being shut up in a black hole. God, don't let her die; I'll pray all day tomorrow. Sister Marie arrives, carrying a tray of little burning coals, like incense. They turn on all the lights. Christiane, very red, her cheeks swollen, grabs at Sister Marie's arm like an animal. She forgives her. "There, breathe in slowly, my child," she says to her. Her hair falls onto the tray, over her hands and medals, like the beautiful saints. Now her breathing is quiet, her head on the pillow is peaceful. They take her tray away. I see Christiane in the dark. Maybe she's dead now. I'll have seen a saint from the city of Jean Bart die. I'm going to pray for her soul. The sisters are talking in hushed tones.

No one says anything to *me*. The damp sheets are sticking to me. Christiane didn't die. Maybe she'll die tonight, without a sound. The dead are silent. I'm afraid and I shiver in my bed. And suddenly there's no air . . . I'm breathing fast, I'm suffocating, I'm going to scream. But I'm not really suffocating. In my ears I hear the sound of the sea.

Sister puts her cool hand on my cheek and says good morning, with the thermometer in her hand. There's no need to hurry in the morning at the infirmary. I walk slowly to the toilet. I like to dawdle, it gives me time to think of other things. They say I daydream. There's a mirror there. I see Christiane in it. She's put her hair up in a net and is dressed in a long gown like a lady. I don't have a temperature anymore, it's too bad. Over coffee, Christiane asks me what's the matter and smiles at me the way she did in the refectory. It's funny, she's forgotten how she suffered last night. I tell her I've had a high temperature, it will come back again tonight. She reads as she eats. I'd like to ask her whether she wets her feet when she crosses a stream, like St. Bernadette.

But I don't dare. She eats, keeping her mouth properly closed. Then she shuts her eyes and goes to sleep. I don't interest her.

The doctor comes with his bag, Sister Marie follows him. He looks at my throat with a stick because the pain is way down . . . in the larynx . . . He pats my cheek and says, "There, there, my child, you mustn't get excited!" His raincoat smells of wine and the Métro in Paris. He's tall. He's a man. The doctor, without uttering a word, takes command of the sisters and everyone else.

He touches us wherever he pleases and sits down just like that, no matter where, without looking. They've put a screen around Christiane's bed because you're not supposed to see a big girl without her clothes on. The doctor listens to her heart. They give me some water to gargle with. I make bubbles in my throat without swallowing and spit like the refugees in rue des Jardins Saint-Paul. The doctor leaves with his bag, without shutting the door.

I slept on my rosary and the little cross came off. I'll have to look at some holy pictures and pray.

Josette has arrived; she's often sick because of the shadow on her lung. She coughs; that must give her a fever. They put a tray down near her bed full of little glass jars. Cupping glasses! Josette lifts her nightgown under the covers. Sister Gabrielle lights the cupping glasses and fixes them to her back. You can see a circle of red flesh in each one, the same as at the butcher's. The glasses knock against each other when she moves. Two have already broken. I can't help laughing. It's so funny, a back full of cupping glasses.

When Sister leaves, Christiane says, "We're going to play beggar-my-neighbor!" and she makes the cards slide and jump against each other very fast in her hand, like a magician. Then she says, "Cut!" and Josette, who's sitting on her bed, makes two stacks. They draw to see who begins. They beggar their neighbor with cards that have two heads and no feet. The king is higher than the queen and she can take the knave. Christiane has all the aces; that gives her the advantage and she wins two games. Josette complains, she coughs. "Please, Christiane, I want my revenge!" "Gladly," she answers in a serious voice.

Josette cried a lot the other day when the mail was given out. Her mother had written her that her father was a prisoner in Germany. Adèle's father had also been taken prisoner, he was an officer in the Marines. We have a lot of prisoners of war right now. We say prayers in chapel for their return: "Lord Jesus, sweet hope of France . . ." And we sing a special hymn: "For all the prisoners of war over there far from home . . ." There's also a nice song, the one about the little girl who writes, "Oh, Daddy, when you come home what a beautiful day . . . !" But it's not always all right when they come back. We know a story that really happened.

Once a prisoner escaped from his camp. He was coming back in a gay mood, by way of the Jura Mountains, whistling as he went along the path. No one in his family knew; he was going to surprise them. The courtyard was dark because of the war. Unfortunately, that day they'd forgotten to close the cesspool. He fell in, poor fellow! It was only the next day when they were stirring the dung with a pitchfork that it caught onto his clothes.

We look disgusted when we hear the story, even though we know it by heart.

Jesus will soon be born on Christmas Day to redeem us. We learn about his birth in catechism; it's the most important holiday before Easter. We don't believe in a Santa Claus anymore who comes down through a hole in the chimney and puts presents in our shoes—they're just silly stories. When you're a Christian you can't believe in just anything. I pray to the Blessed Virgin for Jesus to enlighten me. Beware of silliness and bad thoughts. I feel full of love for Jesus. When I pray in bed at night, I ask him to make me a saint.

The Son of God was born in a manger because there was no place for him at the inn in Bethlehem. I make a nice manger for him in my locker. Sister Marie is going to inspect it. The best one will get a prize. I work hard at it. When we go to the park, I pull up some moss growing at the foot of the trees. It's very cold outside and it makes your hands shake; you have to be careful not to tear the moss. My hands are blue with chilblains and they're covered with green from the sticky moss. I'm doing a good deed. I've taken everything out of my locker, even my doll from Paris. I tossed her into my locker alongside my old shoes. She doesn't count anymore now that I'm a Christian. I think about her sometimes; I'd like to dress her up, but I'm ashamed to. We spread out our moss and start cleaning it on the courtyard floor near our lockers. There are lots of little beasts underneath it, not the Good Lord's creatures—pesky insects. For the rocks in the manger, I take some brown wrapping paper and sit on it to flatten out the creases—the rocks in the hills of Judea are smooth. I cut the ox and ass out from some pictures. To make the shepherds who received the good tidings, I tear a page out of a book. The Infant Jesus is the little celluloid boy-doll that was in my last package. I don't get packages anymore. No one has said anything to me, but I know: my mother's not in Paris anymore, I'm sure of it. And I don't know where she is. I don't want to think about it. My mother's not a French mamma. She doesn't write anymore. I've had one letter and I think it's from my aunt. Her concierge wrote it for her. I cut off a lock of my hair to make a pretty Jesus. The Blessed Virgin is holding up well, kneeling in the moss to adore her son—because I cut her out of cardboard. But I can't keep Joseph on his knees, he falls down all the time, and the rocks won't stop wobbling at the bottom of the manger. I suddenly feel like tearing the whole thing up, but I control myself. I want to win the prize. Really, I feel like chucking it all . . . The string holding the divine star the Three Wise Men are going to follow has snapped in two. And the pesky insects are still in the moss, even though I keep catching them and crushing them underfoot.

I've brought back some fresh moss and run to my locker. Martine bumps into me from behind. "See what you've done, you've crushed my moss!" I tell her I didn't do it on purpose . . . but her moss is ruined. She looks at me, her hands on her hips. She looks pretty mean like that. You shouldn't try to resist mean people when they're angry. I think of the left cheek, the Lord's. I want to tell her, "Go ahead, hit me!" I don't have the courage. People are looking at us. I hold my cheek out all the same . . . That'll surprise her! She's so furious she hits me, she pulls my hair! And then, I'm not sure why, I grab her calf and bite it; I pinch her thighs with both hands. My left cheek is burning and Jesus' words are ringing in my ears: "Love thy neighbor as thyself!" All's lost, I can't stop myself anymore. I start to run, my foot gets tangled in the moss, and I fall flat on my face on the cement. I hear laughter. My knee's bleeding; I run outside and limp toward the chestnut tree. I pick up some pebbles and start to work off my rage. The roots of the chestnut tree are entwined like snakes and reach as far as the benches. I feel tears rising in my throat . . . I scratch the earth with a stick and uncover an ant hill. I strike at it. Ants run out from all sides, forming a circle. How stupid they are! I squash one. "There, that'll teach you!" I say out loud as I wipe the blood off my knee. Another one, a big one, moves ahead with a white bundle on its back; I know it's been preparing it all summer. I flick it off my finger —it's so small—and say, "The ant is not a lender!" as Yvonne, the little girl from Marseilles does.

She arrived at the château with the last train before they were bombed. Her parents are rich and she has very good manners. She learned a lot of animal stories in their candy store. She tells them to us whenever we ask. She doesn't say anything else, she just recites stories. She's little, my age. As she talks, she always clenches a fistful of candied fruit from her shop in Marseilles. At first we didn't understand her stories, because she tells them so slowly, without a pause, in a Marseilles accent. At the end of "Master Crow" the rest of us repeat after her, "This lesson is well worth the cheese, no doubt." Then, standing still, with her serious storyteller's look, she stuffs a handful of candied fruit in her mouth. Still chewing, she starts all over again with "The Crow and the Fox." I still look for crows in the trees, but I have never seen a fox.

At mail time, noon, everyone was reading letters from home in hushed voices to themselves, when suddenly there was an enormous silence. We all turned around. Henriette had stood up. I couldn't see her face, but the others said her eyes were red. She was holding a letter which she put in her pocket as she walked out the door. She left without permission. Mademoiselle Laure looked at her without a word. No one has ever dared to leave before grace. "What's the matter with her?" Christiane said. Henriette went out toward the park.

I was thinking so hard about Henriette, while I was taking my nap under the courtyard roof, that I couldn't pray. She hasn't come back. What can have happened to her? Where is she? I'm afraid she has run away. The paths are covered with snow. She must have a big secret and be very unhappy. During recess, I'm too upset to play. Without asking permission, before Sister can see me, I run to the Avenue in the park.

There are some footprints in the snow. I look at the outlines left by her shoes, but I don't dare walk in Henriette's footprints. I'd like to fly like a bird. I take light, light steps, our footprints in the snow—Henriette's and mine! I follow hers to the intersection, near the grotto of the Blessed Virgin. I'm afraid of seeing her. But I go on looking for her. I read once, in a book about the Cossacks, that when they were looking for someone on the road they'd put their ear to the ground to listen, so they'd know which way the person had gone. I've lost Henriette's tracks. I'm cold. My eyes hurt so much, all around it's so white with the snow and glare. Just before the grotto, I hear a little noise . . . I don't dare go farther. She's there, under the little stone porch between the trees! I hope she hasn't seen me! My heart's beating fast. Oh, Henriette! I'd like so much to . . . I call very softly, "Henriette, Henriette!" and run toward the courtyard. Sister Anne catches me coming through the door. "Where were you, mademoiselle? Who gave you permission to go out without your coat? We've been looking for you. Go to the parlor immediately!"

Sister Marie points, from her armchair, to a special letter for me on her desk—a letter from my father. He's in Palestine, as usual, and he has printed twenty-five words on a piece of yellow paper with lines. It's marked TELEGRAM and in small letters underneath *Cairo–Red Cross, Service of His Majesty the King*. Sister Marie explains that I have to answer in the same way, with twenty-five words—not more—because of the war. She asks me what I want to say to him. I don't know, I really don't need him anymore. Then I say—also because I want to please Sister Marie; she'll see that in my soul I'm a real Christian—that I want his permission to be baptized. Aside from that, I have nothing to say to my father. He's an engineer. I've only seen him in photos; the nicest one is where he's with my mother, in color, before I was born. Their heads are touching. Aunt Ida told me that in Russia our family was very rich before they took all their factories away.

In bed that night I say my prayers with my wooden crucifix over my heart and my hands crossed on top. I can't wait to think about Henriette. I haven't seen her since the park. But I still see her in my mind, under the stone porch between the tall white trees . . . and our footprints in the snow . . .

Then I find myself transported to a great sunny plain, together with Henriette. We travel all through France and, after that, across the mountains beyond the Pyrenees. I follow her to protect her from danger; she holds my hand. She's wearing a queenly robe and a crown, a glistening wreath I made for her. She's radiant. I am her servant and her disciple. I smooth her path and remove the pebbles from under her feet. The two of us walk lightly along in the sun, singing my favorite hymn: "Flowers of Israel . . . look from heaven and hear our prayer . . ." When we get to the desert, I kneel down and wash her tired feet with warm sand. Then I fit her with fine lambskin slippers and sprinkle precious perfume on her hair. She smiles at me. She will tell me her secret because I am her well-beloved disciple. She will know me and I will serve her till the end of my days—I swear it. We're both descended from the Ancient People. Oh, Henriette, I'll feel proud with you! I'll knock on doors; we'll spread the good word and people will know us. Oh, God! I feel feverish, my hands are clammy, my mind's wandering. I don't want to be sick for Christmas.

The next day, as I walked behind Christiane in the snow, I heard her telling one of the seniors that Henriette had received a letter from her girl friend. Her parents and her two older brothers had been deported. Someone had informed against them. They're no longer in France. I ask myself whether it's the same thing they used to say at home in Paris, rue des Jardins Saint-Paul: "They've been taken away!" When I saw

Henriette again, in line, I didn't dare go up and ask her. She never confides in anyone, except maybe Christiane. A girl friend writes her letters. *I* don't have any friends. I think of my mother. I don't hear from her at all anymore. Maybe she's been deported, too, like Henriette's mother. But since I want to become a nun, and afterward a saint, I won't need a family anymore.

We've almost finished our preparations for Christmas. We've been given new clothes for winter. And some presents have come for us from Rome. During the last few days, we've heard some good stories and a Breton legend. Christmas Eve the pink pavilion is all lit up and we feast there on the most delicious dish: pork. All during naptime that afternoon, we hear the squeals of hogs being slaughtered in the village. It's sad hearing them die—but animals don't have souls; the meat is very fat, you eat it with mashed potatoes. We all look very pretty—each of us is wearing her best outfit. I'm wearing my pleated skirt and the sweater my mother knitted, but I've just stained it. Dessert is a surprise wrapped in silver paper: a crêpe. In memory of the poor Breton servant who stayed home alone to make crêpes while the faithful went to Mass. The Blessed Virgin appeared before her in the kitchen. A miracle!—it's better than Midnight Mass! *I* haven't had a vision yet, but I'm waiting.

At grace, when everyone gets up, I remain seated with my glass of milk. Sister Anne is watching me. I don't like milk with cream in it, it's sticky. Everyone here likes it. In the morning, when Sister Marie leaves, they fight beside the empty milk jug over who's going to scrape the hardened cream hanging over the edge like yellow strips of cloth. Everyone's standing up singing and I'm still sitting down. Oh, if only that glass of milk would disappear the way things do in fairy tales . . . the milk dances away . . . my head is spinning . . . it's a miracle. I find myself transported to the bathroom with Sister Anne, who had forced me to drink. I throw up my whole Christmas dinner.

I'm afraid of missing Midnight Mass. Sister looks at me and says, "My child, you're white as a sheet!" And I repeat with my lips, "Sheet . . . sheet . . ."

"Everyone up, Jesus is born!" Sister Marie turns all the lights on. It's midnight! The church bells in the village are ringing for Christmas. I dress quickly, repeating to myself the new Latin hymns, because I'm going to be in the choir. Outside, the path that leads from the château to the chapel is covered with little lanterns; there's fresh snow. We, the faithful, walk close together, as they do in the hymn; also, because it's very cold and we can see our breath. I'm very frightened as we go by the Gallic hut. The fir trees in the park make big dark shadows. I run from one group to another so I won't be alone in the emptiness of the dark night. The searchlight on the Germans' tower turns in a circle.

The chapel has never been so beautiful. It's all lit up for the glory of the Christ Child. Rows of candles are burning before the altar. They dazzle your eyes when you look at them flickering on the purple and white banners. The bells are pealing: it is midnight and Christ is born. The priest's chasuble glitters with gold ornaments in the shape of the cross. It's a little crooked because he has to keep moving for the service. The crèche—a real one—is on one side, with the Holy

Family and the animals in it. But as we're singing the hymn in chorus, I see another crèche ten times bigger and more beautiful: *"Transeamus quem Bethlehem . . . Et cum videamus . . . laudate . . ."* The shepherds rush forward, thousands of stars appear, and the Three Kings carry gold and incense . . . *"Gloria, gloria . . ."* The archangel's trumpet rings out. *"Gloria . . . in excelsis Deo . . ."* Then a great silence. All you hear is the sacred music of the organ. After that, our voices take up the tremendous round again. As we're singing, a big hole opens in the sky so that you see all the important saints, covered with haloes of fire, sitting on God's right. They sing the glory of the Son with us. The girls who are receiving communion take Jesus in their hearts. I envy them.

In the refectory, I sit on the radiator and look out the window at the falling snow. You have to move fast if you're going to keep warm. As soon as lunch is over, I rush to get a place on the radiator; there aren't enough. Paulette, the orphan, is next to me, knitting. Through the mist and snow, you can see little chalets with red chimneys rising over the hills, like the Christmas cards the others receive in the mail. But here in the country we have nothing. Not even a lake. There's a pretty one in the song we danced to yesterday: "The snow cloud has emptied its flakes; it scatters white gulls on the lake . . . and the lake is so pretty, it's snowing white gulls . . ." It's a pity for the sparrows who die from the cold. I hear the gurgling of the radiator; it burns my behind a little.

Downstairs, they're letting out war cries. We play war a lot these days. Christiane and Adèle are the generals defending the Maginot Line; the Germans and English advance. They fire cannons and guns at each other, and yell and run about; they're as rowdy as boys. The girls from Dunkirk sing, "Happiness entered my heart when Hitler entered Belgium; he told me he needed forty-five minutes to get to the British Isles . . ." Then the Parisians answer, "Come, little Fritz, if you want to take a bath, the English . . ." The Marshal's soldiers have won. Christiane organizes all the games with her friends from Dunkirk—they're tough!

On letter-writing day, since I don't write anymore, I study the life of St. Teresa. She's very beautiful and died not such a long time ago. On the first page—it's not a drawing, it's a real photo—she's wearing a long black veil. A crucifix with flowers is over her heart, and her hands—they're very white—are crossed on top. Her pure eyes are looking straight ahead. When she was very little she had long hair with white bows on both sides. She was very devout; she had visions and her ardent heart urged her to make sacrifices. Seriously ill, she gave herself entirely to the Lord and offered him her suffering. She stung herself with nettles. That's too much, I tell myself, and I stop reading. I'd thought of nettles and she'd already done it. It was my idea and I thought I was the only one to have it.

I lose my page; putting the book down, I watch the others writing their parents. Germaine is drawing a heart. She makes little red dots. She says it's blood because of love. Then she draws an arrow—"a sword that pierces the heart." Jesus said that a good heart is the only thing that counts for getting into heaven. Like everyone else, my heart bleeds for the martyred saints when it's supposed to, but the truth is, I don't feel my heart. Except in bed at night when I pray with my little wooden cross. I press it against my heart until it hurts.

The sound of thunder, followed by a long whistling noise, makes my bed shake. I open my eyes, it's dark. The night light has gone out, but it turns on and off again several times. Everyone's awake and shouting. Thérèse's bed has slid to the middle of the dormitory; I can barely see her. I ask her what's going on: "It's an air raid!" The windows bang, an acrid odor of smoke stings my throat. Sister Marie and Mademoiselle Laure come in carrying paraffin lamps. They order us to be quiet, and we kneel down and recite the creed to ward off danger. We're very frightened. But the air raid is over and I haven't heard a thing! It's a very small, rural air raid. And here in the château, with the big park wall surrounding us with God, we don't have to be afraid. Jacqueline says she saw a huge ball of fire coming down from heaven.

I remember in Lorris, when my mother and I were in hiding, I saw a real-war air raid. Everyone fled. We were living in a little house beside the road and all the refugees—there were so many of them!—were sleeping in carts, trucks, and cars. One day I looked outside; the planes had passed very low, with a big roar. The refugees along the road all rushed into our little house, bumping and shoving each other. My mother pushed me into the other room under the bed and locked the door. The floor and walls were shaking from all the loud noise. The glass in the windows and the tiles fell down. I stuffed my ears. I thought the bombs were falling on us. My mother clasped me in her arms; we were going

to die! There were huge explosions and horses screaming outside. My head was touching the bedsprings; it
hurt, but I didn't dare move.

For a long time we went on hearing the screams of
the horses, then nothing more. My mother opened the
door. The refugees came out from under the table. It's
funny to see grownups on all fours with big frightened
eyes. Outside, thick clouds of stinging green smoke hung
in the air. I saw a cart upside down, and the horse attached to it lying on his side, his stomach ripped open
and quivering, full of blood; one leg had been crushed.
He didn't move. My mother put her hands over my
eyes. But I'd already seen it. We ran away through the
smoke with all the others down the main street. People
were fleeing with bundles along the highway, toward
Montargis and the Sully bridge. The houses near the
town hall had big holes in them; I thought of a little
girl who had lots of mechanical dolls. We could go to
her house and take them. People were going into places
everywhere; just like that, the doors were open. They
took whatever they wanted. It's permitted during air
raids. Alongside the school, where the soldiers had
camped, people were saying, "Those fellows ran away.
Stark naked without even their boots!" A man was holding a pair of pants and shaking them. He searched
through the pockets and took out a notebook and some
string. I took a pair of pants, too. All I found was a pipe.
But I had no use for a pipe. I was looking for a
harmonica and a doll. That evening, the mayor gave an
order announced by the local police drummer that
people must bring everything they'd found to the town
hall. My mother and I hadn't found anything worth
bothering about, but we went to the town hall anyway.

They gave us a card for me to buy galoshes. After that, the Germans came and restored order. All the refugees had left.

The next day, the château carpenter, standing on a ladder propped against the dormitory window, replaces the broken panes. We watch him cutting the squares of glass. Josette describes the air raid in Belfort: "The whole city was destroyed." I look beyond, and all the way to the horizon. I know that there are villages in France that have been bombed by the enemy. That's very sad: France is the most beautiful country in the world. At vespers we sing, "Lord Jesus, sweet hope of France . . ." The incense rises toward the altar in homage to our country, humiliated by the enemy.

Nothing was destroyed in our château, it's like a fortress. And, of course, we have the Germans' tower to protect us. We had a good laugh when Mademoiselle Laure described how the Germans made a mistake and fired on each other. The plane that did the bombing crashed on the road along the Saône.

It has stopped raining. The river is in flood. The water has reached almost to the ramparts of the park. It's spring; we go for a walk in double file, marching and singing: "There're no wooden legs in the army . . . The best way to march . . ." I wanted the villagers to see us all singing and marching in such an orderly fashion. It's the first time we've left the château. The line breaks up, we start skipping. The Saône has flooded the fields all the way to the road; in the distance, where the water and sky touch, it looks like the sea. Martine throws a pebble. It cuts the air, skims over the water, and, after several bounces, slowly makes the still water open its sleeping eyes. After a long while, the eyes narrow and the water goes back to sleep. It looks so easy. But my pebble sinks right away in its hole. The sun makes the water sparkle, the clouds set in it. We've found some fragments of the plane. Thérèse keeps two as souvenirs. I touch them—they feel hard and sharp. I put one in my pocket; it makes a hole as I walk. I'm afraid the wind will bring the water over to where we are. Sister says the Saône has overflowed its banks. You can't see it anymore, it seems to have all spilt over onto the fields. It's a deluge. God promised not to make any more floods; the rainbow is the proof.

Irene leans over to wash a piece of wreckage from the plane. You can see the reflections of her hair, all frizzy, in the water; thick layers of black and golden curls. They say her grandmother was a black woman from the colonies. She arrived at the château with the same convoy as the girls from Dunkirk. Irene is from Lille. We admire her hair, everyone wants to comb it. I touch my own hair. I'd like still to be the only one with curly hair.

A peasant passes with his dog. He takes his cap off when he sees Sister Anne and looks at the water. Some of the girls pat the dog; he doesn't mind but Sister scolds them. When the farmer and the dog leave, she tells us that they've gone to look at the damage done to his ruined wheatfields. The Angelus rings. It's a bell far away from our château. We stop to meditate, our hands joined. I'm cold. I shut my eyes to hide the great empty stretch of water and the gray sky: I see God and our chapel. The dog is barking in the distance. We see them, the man and his dog, go toward the village; they're going home to their house. As for us, we go back to the château. I'm glad. It's good to be in our park again. The lights twinkle in the chapel; I touch the smooth wood of the prayer bench; yellow flowers decorate the altar. I'm happy, every day of my life will be like this. And a day will come when I'll get the call and belong to God.

In the refectory, I look at myself in the pumpkin soup and make bounces along the surface with my spoon. Thérèse has colored the pieces of plane wreckage red, with a brush, and marked the date. It is 1943.

The iron gate is open to let in the new girls from Paris. Big girls. One of them is carrying a pretty red suitcase, her name is Carmen. She's seventeen. Everyone looks at her. The first day, she outshines Christiane, our team captain, at game time, by taking all the prisoners. She also likes to play the buffoon, and we follow all her orders. Parisians are very proud. Best of all, Carmen has long black hair, and her eyes move around like butterflies. She wears pretty dresses and no smock, and shoes with straps. She tells stories like grownups and gypsies. They say her parents are Spanish.

On our walk in the park, she takes Sister Marie's arm, with the other girls gathered around. You can hear what they say as you follow; I watch Carmen walking in her pretty white sandals. She says, "If you only knew!" She was walking up the Eiffel Tower with a group of boys. They'd got to the second floor, the wind was blowing between the iron rungs, when a girl climbed right past them in a pleated skirt. All of a sudden a violent gust of wind threw her skirt over her head. She didn't have any pants on. We stifled our laughter. Sister Marie didn't say anything, but I saw her lip tremble. Carmen shakes her long earrings with a toss of her head and begins another story. Her hair is swept up into a tall black tower, kept in place by golden barrettes. Then she tells a riddle and asks us if we want to give up: "Sitronpressé . . . after an air raid, what is it?" Some of us think she means *citron pressé*, squeezed lemon; you make lemonade out of it by adding sugar. But no, it's *six troncs pressés*, six torsos without heads or legs lying heaped on top of one another. Everyone bursts into laughter . . .

During an inspection of our lockers, Sister Marie confiscated some of Carmen's books. She had the nerve to say, "What! I'm not free to read what I want!" Sister Marie ordered her to follow her to the parlor. She probably got a good hiding.

Since then, she hasn't told any more stories. She acts very pious in chapel. Now that the weather's good, we have gym over by the tennis court. Carmen turns cartwheels. You can see her shorts under her skirt; her earrings and her long hair fall upside down as she turns in the wheel. Now there are several girls rolling in the grass, their legs spread apart. I tried, too, with no success. I can't even do a head stand with my feet against the wall; it scares me to see the sky upside down. Carmen braided her long hair and made herself a crown; then she climbed the fir tree and swung from a branch. In the evening, she danced the "Blue Danube . . ."

All the girls who are knitting sit in a corner of the courtyard. Thérèse showed me how to knit plain. I found some yarn in an empty locker and I sing along with them as I knit: "Gypsy with the big black eyes, your hair the color of night and the luster of your dark skin . . ." We think of Carmen. My mother used to sing that song, too, in Paris, when she was cleaning house. I haven't enough yarn to finish anything. I undo what I've started and begin again in purl stitch. We also sing some new love songs we've learned, pronouncing the words in a slow, languorous voice: "Rocked by the silvery waves . . . I want to sleep on your heart and dream . . ." After that it's the song of a guard who's late: "Young lady, wait for his return . . ." We write down the words so as to learn them by heart: "A doll was born in Java as pretty as a jewel . . . We adore her, we're crazy about her . . . !" They dance the Java in couples, Carmen and Colette show them the steps. Henriette doesn't join in, she has other concerns; she has taken her piece of canvas from her locker and is embroidering. Henriette—nobody can outshine Henriette, she's still our great captain.

Just before bed, Carmen puts on a show: "Bluebeard." She puts on a real beard, her face is frightful, and we are very scared. Another time, we turned the lights off and Carmen put on a tragedy: "John the Baptist and Salome." We were screaming with horror: John the Baptist's tongue was hanging out, the real tongue of a shoe. When Sister Anne left and Mademoiselle Eugénie was in charge, Carmen did a belly dance on top of the soup-pot table. She wriggled her hips, waving her hands in the air; the bottom ends of her blouse were knotted over her belly. Adèle said it was a dance from Algiers. Carmen sang an Arab song, clapping her hands to the music. Christiane remarked, "She's a weird one!"

When it began to get warmer, Carmen wanted to take sunbaths on the lawn with her friends. She told us she used to go to the beach with a group of boys in a car. Christiane said to her, "No, that's going too far!" Carmen turned her back, shouting. "What a lot of idiots there are in this dumb place!" I like Christiane, she's devout.

Nowadays I sleep in the little green room they call an alcove, right next to the seniors' dormitory. I can hear them whispering behind the partition. Mademoiselle Agnès, the new novice, monitors us from behind the screen. She has black hair like Carmen, but done up in a net; they're going to cut it off later. She has to take her vows after two years of proving her devotion; then she'll have to vow fidelity to Jesus, whom she'll marry. Still, she plays with us a lot and laughs. The sisters never join us in our games. Mademoiselle Agnès even eats with us. When I get the call someday, I'm going to abstain from all these things. Mademoiselle Agnès teaches us to dance to sacred tunes. She was raised in a convent. She has the voice of an angel. She's very strict and looks down on little girls who are timid.

One night I went all the way to the seniors' bathroom. The door was bolted. I was scared. I heard voices. Someone was inside. They opened it. It was Carmen and some seniors who were reading under the little white light over the toilets. Carmen, raising her lace sleeve, said, "What on earth are you doing here?" Really, I didn't know. They were all in their nightgowns, sitting on the toilet seats with books in their hands. Carmen, touching her curlers, added, "Get out of here, you little sneak!" So then I went to the juniors' bathroom. That will teach me! *Henriette* reads books with no pictures in them on the bench in the courtyard.

I shut my eyes and here I am with her in the valley of the sun. We walk together toward a faraway country. Then we go to the mountains and pick flowers; I go ahead of her to remove the thorns. Afterward, we go down to the desert; the tempter will come and I'll chase him away. We'll fast until sunset. In the evening, we'll go in the water of the river, up to our knees. She will baptize me. I am not worthy to do the same for her, not even to tie her shoelaces. An angel will come to warn us of danger. I'll find a refuge for the two of us . . . Henriette sits on a bank and meditates. I've brought some moss to make a soft cushion. She's thinking of secret things. It's not yet the right moment to reveal them to me. Then I stand guard to protect her should any suspicious strangers try to bother her.

When we reach St. Joseph's oratory we turn and go back. It's odd, we only walked half the way today. A line of trucks, covered with foliage, is stationed in the great Avenue, near the chapel. Some soldiers are living there; they arrived last night, without a sound. They're carrying basins of hot water from the kitchen and we stand back to make way for them. Their heavy shoes crunch the gravel. They're not wearing boots like real German soldiers. A group of them are standing there doing nothing; they watch us as they roll up their sleeves. One of them laughingly raises his cap to us. We run away. We've been told not to go near them; we watch them from a distance. We're forbidden to go to the part of the Avenue where the trucks are. Every day they wash in our showers.

You hear them running early in the morning. They do calisthenics: "One two . . . one two . . . !" Carmen went to see them, accompanied by a group of seniors. She was wearing a big white ribbon and her hair fell over her shoulders. She lifted her hand to say "Hi!" jingling the little bells on her bracelet. Christiane says that she's depraved and that she likes men. She keeps photos of actresses in her pocket. Carmen spoke to one of the soldiers; none of the monitors saw her. Some of the others went over to say hello. We, the juniors, followed them. The soldiers beckoned to us and whistled, putting two fingers in their mouths. One of them took a yoyo out of his pocket and bounced it back and forth very high. But the seniors pushed us behind, the sisters arrived, and we ran away.

The seniors curl their hair now and put flowers in it. They never stop repeating, "Attention!" Ever since the trucks and soldiers arrived, it's not the same anymore. During Mass and at vespers, even when you can't hear them, you know they're nearby, you think of having fun with them.

At lunch, Sister Marie and our Mother Superior, Marie-Louise Cortin, gave us a lecture. We received strict orders not to speak to the soldiers or go near the part of the Avenue where their trucks are stationed. Any act of disobedience would be severely punished. That afternoon the seniors only stood and looked from a distance. The soldiers waved to them. One of them called, "Carmen."

Henriette plays checkers with Christiane. Some of the girls crowd around. Henriette thinks a long time before moving her piece; silent, never taking her eyes off the board, she takes the first piece. They're at the beginning of the game. I like to play checkers but I move fast, without stopping to think. I haven't the patience to concentrate on several pieces at the same time. Still, it's not just a game of chance; you have to calculate your moves. I try to prepare one for Henriette. I've noticed an empty square and three checkers.

She can take them and get a queen. Suddenly I see my finger pointing to Henriette's side of the board, but she pushes my hand away, looking slightly annoyed; then says kindly, "Don't touch, little one!" I move farther away on the bench; the blood rushes to my cheeks and I lower my head.

The trucks and soldiers left during the night. They left long trenches, full of paper and empty boxes, in the Avenue. We've been ordered to fill them in with earth; we work with both hands. Closing my eyes, I see myself back again at Berck Beach, next to my mother. I mash the sand and make sand pies. But I mustn't waste time like this. Everyone's worried. Carmen has disappeared!

We don't know whether she ran away or whether the soldiers took her away with them. What a scandal! The senior girls whisper to each other. The police have come from the department of Haute-Saône to make an on-the-spot investigation. The sisters and our Mother Superior are all gathered under the big oak tree near the chapel and have been drinking tea, sitting in the wicker armchairs. It's because Carmen has turned out badly. Sister Marie had to keep back all the curious girls crowding around to see what was in her locker. She found *The Mysteries of Paris*. That evening Christiane played "Bluebeard" exactly the way Carmen had, dressed in trousers. Sister Marie came in and told her this was forbidden. In the future, she said, we will be more carefully watched and everything will return to normal.

In catechism, we had a sermon on good conduct and adulteresses. It's in the Ten Commandments, in the line about adultery. We all thought of Carmen. But we never spoke her name. There's no longer a Spanish gypsy at the château. For a long time afterward, we went on telling her stories and singing her songs.

Lent is approaching; we have to prepare for the Passion of Christ and the big day—Easter.

The sun moves past the third Station of the Cross on the windows of our chapel. Jesus falls down, no one helps him; Simon the Cyrene hasn't passed by yet. The red of his coat shines in the sun. The people and his tormentors had mocked him, dressing him up as the king of the Jews. His halo gleams between the points of the spears held by the soldiers, who treat him as though he were one of the thieves. I follow the Mass with the other eye; one must not let oneself be distracted, even by a sacred subject. Our priest bows to the altar and drinks from the chalice. A loud sound of shoes against the bench and the sliding of someone falling limply to the floor bring all heads up. One of the faithful has made a gap in our ranks. Germaine has fainted. Sister Marie rushes to her from her prie-dieu, everyone is looking— but out of the corner of the eye; no one dares turn around, the priest goes on with the Mass. Sister Marie enters the pew, leans over, and, looking distressed, takes Germaine in her arms. She carries her to the sacristy without stopping to genuflect in the aisle. The white coif covers Germaine, who is bent over double, her head hanging down and her face very white.

At the château, someone faints almost every morning during Mass. Not always the same girls. Then Sister Marie—she's a strict saint—takes us in her arms. We are weak and devout. So far, I myself have never fainted. It's almost like dying. Afterward you wake up, and at breakfast you're entitled to a little pat of butter, even in the middle of the week.

I'd like so much to faint on the day of the Passion, Good Friday. God would grant me an exceptional grace. We spend forty days preparing for it; we start doing penance on Ash Wednesday. That's when Jesus went to the Mount of the Olives and began to suffer sorrow and agony. He prayed to God to help him. He was in the garden next to the stream, and his soul became sorrowful unto death. All the disciples had practically abandoned him that night; they'd fallen asleep while the Lord was tasting the bitter cup. In spite of their good intentions, Sister Anne explains, because the spirit is willing but the flesh is weak.

We learn all the Stations of the Cross by heart. They take him to a place called Golgotha and give him gall to drink. Thérèse weeps when Sister shows us the picture of the people pushing the crown of thorns on the Lord's head. And He, the Almighty, lets them beat Him with rods while Pontius Pilate washes his hands. All the little girls have tears in their eyes. I lower my head, I have no tears. But I'm very sad; I look at the floor and in my mind I see all the pain, all the spit and nails better than in the pictures. Truly, I force myself to feel each wound with my heart so that I can feel sadder. Why can't *I* manage to cry? And yet, I should be able to, more than the others, because of Judas, his betrayal, and that ungrateful people. I don't belong to that people anymore, not since I left my mother. I'm not baptized yet, but through prayer and sacrifice I'll gain merit and faith. Henriette doesn't belong to that cursed race anymore, either. But she must know; when I think about it, I sense something that escapes me. She knows a secret of the ancient people of Israel that she's jealously guarding. I'd really like to be in the senior catechism class, I'd be able to hear her speak.

During Lent, the period of penance, we have to do without the things we like. I try to do good deeds so that my sins can be forgiven. Jesus suffered so much for the whole world. I think about it as I walk along the path bordered with cornflowers and daisies. Sister Marie has asked us to pick flowers to decorate the chapel. I'm looking for white periwinkles because they're pure; I'll bring back the biggest bouquet. Just past the grotto of the Blessed Virgin I see a whole lot of them in the thicket, but a clump of nettles prevents me from getting to them. I stop. The moment has come for the great sacrifice. Should I sting myself now? All I have to do is roll up my sleeves. I go closer and smell the nasty wild odor of the nettles. I hesitate. I mustn't waste time, I must pick these periwinkles for the Lord. I run back to Sister Marie's group, which has stopped in front of St. Joseph's oratory. Martine cries, "A snake, a snake!" Terrified, she points under the base of the statue. She'd seen it gliding through the grass. What a fright we had! Christiane assures us that it's a garter snake. A garter snake is big and thick but it's harmless; appearances are deceiving. A real snake, a viper, is thin; its head is triangular. That's how you know it's poisonous. Noah really should have left them in the water. They're the basest of animals. It's because of the serpent that man was driven out of Paradise. We walk close together out of fear and no one picks any flowers. My bouquet is very small. The grass is tall in the little wood and the white periwinkles hide in it. It must be full of snakes, too! I'm running in it. "Lord, help me! I'm picking these flowers for you!" I'm pulling up the stems very fast. You have to pick them long so they'll stand out and look proud in the big vases in the chapel. My hand trembles. I say to myself, "You shameless little coward! Pick the ones with the long stems; slow down!" God, but I'm hot! I thought I saw a snake gliding under the ivy but it's only the roots of a tree. I see the Sacred Heart but it's too far away to protect me from danger. I've never gone so far into the woods. Periwinkles have a way of bending their stems under the grass. It cuts my hand when I pick so fast. "For you, Jesus! Another sacrifice!" The truth is, it doesn't count because I'm afraid. I perspire. Jesus sweated, too, when he carried the cross for the whole world. I run from one periwinkle to another. A snake is about to appear, I'm sure of it, just to tempt me and make me miss a chance for a good deed. He'll bite me if he sees me and I'll die without being baptized . . . I'm alone. No noise anywhere around, only the crackling of twigs under my feet. Then I run as fast as I can to the refectory. I'm saved. I've a big bunch of flowers but I'm the last one back. Sister Marie shakes me by the shoulders: "Mademoiselle, you're out of line and you're late!"

I'm very thirsty, but I'm not going to drink anything till the end of my meal. I control myself a long time in order to make a sacrifice. I look at the water tempting me in the cup. I will resist it. It's deliciously cool— Satan has got inside. The mashed potatoes parch my mouth. It makes the sacrifice all the bigger. Thérèse and Germaine, next to me, don't suspect a thing. *I* have a special relationship with God.

Now that I'm older, I've been assigned, along with

some others, to make the little ones' beds in the morning. I choose the one of the little girl who wets her bed. No one else wants to touch it. It smells bad. I work hard at smoothing the sheets, tucking in the corners as tightly as I can. Mademoiselle Laure says that my bed is a model. I have one fault: I'm slow. I already know two sacrifices and I repeat them every day. When I feel like talking I keep quiet—that makes three. When we go to the park I walk in the shade on purpose. I avoid the sun, it feels so good to get warm—that makes four. For the last several days I've been haunting the place where the nettles are.

Today I prayed with lots of fervor. I have more courage than usual. Like Jesus I say, "May thy will be done!" He didn't flinch before the cup of sorrows. Neither did the saints or all the multitude of Christian martyrs. If I want to become a saint I'll have to acquire merit and then perhaps I'll have earned the right to have visions. I wait until the group accompanying Sister Marie goes farther off in the park. I'm careful of my legs near the thicket. It's only my arms that I intend to sting and then conceal in the sleeves of my sweater. You have to do your good deeds in secret. They'd see my legs right away. For Jesus said, "Do not do like the hypocrites in order that they may be seen by men." But I'm afraid of the day when they weigh us and listen to our hearts. I'll be embarrassed and the doctor won't understand. But maybe Sister Marie will see. Oh, and if she does, I'll really be in luck! I won't undress until Sister Marie insists. She'll be convinced of my saintliness once I take off my undershirt. I think about it as I'm looking at the stems of the horrid nettles, which are so much taller than the other grass. They're stiff and dense in this corner of the thicket. I pull my sweater sleeves up. My arms are shivering. I lean over. As I stretch out my hand, my face is right next to these foul creatures and my nose inhales their nasty odor. For a moment, I have doubts: no one has ever done it before. I touch one of the stems; it has hairs, the smell is suffocating. Quickly I pull it up. It's damp and the green part is sticky. I shut my eyes because of its ugliness. Then—very quickly—because of my doubts—I lash my arm. A stinging, burning sensation goes through me—it's the sacred fire; it slowly mounts to my soul and, on its way, cleanses all my impurities, perhaps even my stain and my mother's origin. It's easily worth ten sacrifices. When I open my eyes I see little white bumps with red haloes around them. "Jesus, for you, little Jesus . . ." I stop the prayer. Jesus said you must not multiply vain words. It hurts. When I pull my sweater down you can't see a thing. The wool is rubbing against my bumps. I run off to join the others. No one suspects anything. Not even Sister Marie, who's a saint. I don't know why I feel uncomfortable, not because of the pain, but for another reason. I think my sacrifice is an affront.

That evening, while I was putting on my nightgown, I could smell the odor of burning nettles. If Sister Marie comes to tuck me in . . . I don't have the cross over my heart the way I usually do. That would be going too far. A short prayer is enough—to the Virgin Mary. The contact of the sheets cools the burning. It is worth a long prayer. But why this uneasiness—it's almost a kind of disgust. I don't dare think about Henriette. It's no use; I can see her mocking eyes. What if she knows, too? But God's the only one who knows. As for the others, it's no concern of theirs. These red and white bumps and the smell—could it be leprosy? What did all those saints and martyrs described in the books do? I'm the St. Thomas type—I have doubts and grace is not given to me. It's the fault of my origins; they stand in the way of my path to sainthood. If only Thérèse would stop snoring for once, I might be able to sleep. Does she make sacrifices? What are they? Her ancestors are French so it's not necessary for her to make atonement.

I have three letters left in my locker and I'm going to keep all three; they have pretty envelopes with linings. Before, I was careless and would lose them. My mother sent them to me. I don't think about her when I look at them, as the others do when they arrange theirs in little bundles with ribbons. But something reminds me of home; it worries me. I take two pages out of the blue envelope with the gray lining; it's the last letter from my mother. I unfold it and look at it a long time without reading it. I don't like reading letters, but I want to keep them. My mother had promised me a package. She never sent it . . . I don't want to think about it anymore because letters from my mother are not something important in religion. Sometimes I go through a moment of weakness, but it's way in the back of my mind; I feel anxious, as though I wanted to cry; I feel too sad to play. I have a dreadful feeling that my mother's not in Paris anymore.

Palm Sunday the priest sprinkles us with a branch of blessed boxwood in order to hasten the Kiss of Peace. During Mass the dove, with an olive branch in its beak, announces the message of peace. The entire week is very holy, but it is the dark day of Good Friday that you think about. I dread that day! The hymn of the Passion is the longest and most sacred of all the hymns; it has twenty couplets plus the refrain. It takes courage to sing it all the way to the end without crying.

I saw the place with the nettles again, in the park. As I look at them from a distance, I say to myself, "They're not so bad, they're the Lord's creatures like all the others." My arm doesn't hurt anymore and my welts are disappearing. But I can't rid myself of the smell.

Sister Marie took my pulse and sent me to the green dormitory. I have a temperature and a stomachache. Geneviève's in bed, too. She gets sick often. She's a very thin little girl from Brittany. She has already fainted four times in chapel. She often puts her hand on her forehead, murmuring, even in the middle of a game, "I have a headache." Then she lifts her eyes to heaven—so far that they disappear under her eyelids, and all that's left is the white. It's not difficult to see that she's going to die soon. Her straight hair is pasted down on her temples; it's surely a sign of weakness. She talks all the time, wheezing her *s*'s. Poor thing, she has no strength. The rest of us feel very sorry for her. She's fated to die soon, whereas *I* am soon going to become a saint. I'm waiting for a sign.

It's annoying because now I really do have a stomachache and the smell of nettles doesn't leave me. I've taken the big catechism, which also contains the most beautiful hymns, to bed with me. I'm learning the hymn of the Passion by heart. It's dreadfully sad but I like to sing it and to hum the refrain over and over again: "He died on this cross to save the world . . ." The tune is so sad you feel like crying in spite of yourself. It's a pretty name, Geneviève; it's the name of a great saint who was the patron of Paris. We celebrated her birthday with a

hymn: "Oh, St. Geneviève . . ." In bed, I leaf through
the hymns and ask Geneviève to sing the Passion with
me. She tells me to leave her alone. She knows stories
about her native region. She's very proud of Brittany.
We can hear the hoarse sirens of the boats crossing the
Saône at noon. It reminds her of the boats in Brest. Brittany has the most beautiful sky in the world; the song
proves it: "Oh, how beautiful my Brittany is, you have
to see it under a gray sky . . . It is more beautiful than
Spain . . ." Geneviève is like me, she's always losing in
the ball games and is the last to be chosen. Too bad
that she has to die soon! At lunch, Geneviève makes a
face when she sees the dessert—some custard tarts, dark
brown on the stop; everyone's very fond of them. She
buries herself under the sheets; she's had more than
enough of telling stories. So I eat her tart to please her.
I'll read the Passion by myself. She feels sick and lies
in bed motionless: it's the sign. I haven't finished the tart
or the hymn of the Passion . . . I feel nauseated and
dizzy. I feel like I'm going to die. I haven't the strength
to cry out and warn them so they'll baptize me. And to
think that my mind was on Geneviève's death! That
will teach me! The same thing happened to the shoemaker in Lorris.

My mother and I often used to go to the shoemaker's,
across from the town hall. I wore out a lot of shoes. I
was silly and amused myself by banging my foot against
the sidewalk. The shoemaker would repair them in front
of the window, on a table full of shoes. In the big bed
near the wall there was a black ball sticking out above
the sheets—it was the head of his wife, who was sleeping. She was seriously ill. The neighbors used to drop in

to say things were bad bacause of the war. The shoe-maker would listen but would go on hammering. He couldn't stop, because he needed to buy all the medicines that were lying on the bedside table. One day, as we were on our way there, we heard a rumor that she was dead. But our shoemaker, since he didn't have enough money to buy a coffin right away, had gone on repairing shoes. He'd been hammering the nails in when he suddenly heard his wife turn around and say, "Stop that banging! You're keeping me awake!" The poor man was so startled that he died on the spot. Then they put him in the coffin that he'd prepared for his wife. It was pitiful at the funeral. My mother and I were there—the last people in the procession because we didn't know the French funeral songs. But nevertheless we were his customers. The parish priest sang with the boys from the school. I remembered the word "David." It's a foreign name, the name of my father in Palestine! You say it over and over in the songs the French sing for the dead. They put him in the earth with a spade. There was no longer a shoemaker in Lorris. Except for his wife; but she couldn't fix old shoes. It was during this time that the Germans arrived. We went back to Paris. There are lots of shoemakers in Paris.

Good Friday is the day you fast the most, the blackest Friday of them all. Glory to the Resurrection! The grownups fast and give up everything to mortify the flesh. I take pains to repeat in proper order all the sacrifices I know. I rise closer and closer to God every day. I feel that I can't rise higher even for this great day of mourning. I pray once more for the suffering of Christ. I tremble at the thought that this afternoon Jesus will be crucified. It's a day of darkness despite the sun out-doors. But one mustn't trust in appearances. The real darkness is in the soul.

After my nap I go to meditate on the steps under the arcade, my back against the chapel wall, away from the wind. The stone feels warm in the sun. I shut my eyes; the rays penetrate my skin. When I open them again I see a lizard on the wall, near a crack. He stays stock-still, stretched out the length of his body. The two of us are warming up. I watch him out of the corner of my eye; if I move he'll run away. We're spying on each other. He must be wary of me and want to stay in the sun alone. I imagine that I'm putting out my hand and stroking his back. The sun feels so good. I'd like to stay here like this, with the lizard, forever. The Angelus rings. At the first ring he darts into the crack.

Silently, black berets on our heads, we tiptoe into the chapel, which is draped in black. Everything re-minds one of the Crucifixion: the empty altar has neither flowers nor candles. Each ornament laments the cruel death of Our Lord, abandoned by all and delivered over by his own people. At three o'clock Jesus expires. That's the most solemn moment of all. The priest then reads his sermon.

"Let the Jews not say, 'We did not kill Christ.' It is true that they delivered Him into the hands of Pilate, the magistrate, but only so that they might appear in some way innocent . . . Pilate was a participant in their crime to the extent of what he did do . . . for he tried, to the best of his ability, to remove Him from their hands . . . He had the Lord scourged, not with the intention of destroying Him, but to satisfy their fury . . . But it is you, O Jews, who really killed Him."

No doubt about it, I thought. And everything that happened later to this people was no more than they deserved!

The faithful bow their heads and meditate. Then we quietly start singing the sweetest, most sorrowful of all the Latin hymns: *"Parce domine, parce populo tuo . . . ne in aeternum . . ."* For a long time we remain stricken with grief by the Latin hymn. The altar has become dark, you can barely make out the priest's chasuble. It's the first time that I approach the holy table; not to take communion, I still do not have the right to do that, but to kiss the fragment of the true cross of Jerusalem. The priest holds it out to me—to me, a descendant of the people who crucified the Son of God. He looks at me, his eyes full of Christian charity. I am forgiven. His hand trembles as he holds the relic near my lips. In my silent prayer, nevertheless, I say, "Lord, I am not worthy of this honor; I am guilty through this people. Take pity on me!" I am sad. One cannot erase the traces or stains of one's origins. Never to be like everyone else! But a new, confused feeling steals over me and makes me lift my head in pride. Henriette is different, too; could it be for the same reason? She, too, is descended from this people, but she probably comes from the chosen people, whereas I'm from the accursed.

If only I could faint and suffer; pale and devout, I would atone on the altar for both of us, for the crimes of our ancestors. Germaine's back, as she bends over in sad meditation, is curved into a hump. The doctor has prescribed ladder exercises for her.

At the end of the park we have a large garden which supplies us with vegetables—the kitchen garden. The path that leads to it is sprinkled with forget-me-nots all the way to the poultry yard. They're such pretty little flowers but humble; they hide under the grass. I leave the group to search for some near the bushes. I stop at the sound of murmuring voices. Perhaps they're strangers. Frightened, I walk around the bush toward an opening. I distinctly hear, "Here, swallow this one!" I push aside some branches and find myself in a clearing in front of Paulette, the orphan, her head thrown back, her hands at her mouth: she's sucking an egg. Martine, a needle in her hand, is piercing another. They both jump back startled when they see me. Paulette—the white of the raw egg still on her lips—says to me as she throws away the shell, "Why are you looking at us like that?" She drops her voice: "You're not going to report us, are you?" I don't know what to say; I'm simply astonished to see all those empty eggshells on the ground. It's a long time since I've seen any—not since I left Paris. Several times Sister Stanislas, our Polish cook, who dresses all in white, brought me an omelet in a frying pan to eat in the refectory because I'm underweight. Everyone looked at my plate: we never have eggs at the château. It's peculiar to make holes in an egg and gobble it all down on the sly. But I can see they want me to leave. "If you steal an egg you'll steal a cow!"

Jesus is risen! This is how we start the day of rejoicing. So that that which is written may be fulfilled: After the third day Christ will leave his tomb to establish the Church. In the morning we do one another's hair so that we'll be beautiful. Joy and sunlight pervade the festive château. We're on our way to Easter Mass to take communion—except Henriette and me. At this High Mass, everyone pays attention and no one faints, for the body and the blood of Christ give it double importance. Our priest is dressed in white and gold and the chapel is filled with the sweet scent of flowers. So much joy distracts me from my meditation. At the bottom of my heart—I don't dare say it, but I prefer it when things are sad. We're going to get two portions of butter for breakfast. I'm going to give one of them to Germaine. It's not every day I get a chance to make such a sacrifice . . . We come to the greatest hymn of all, the most triumphant, which glorifies the King of Kings: *Christus vincit, Christus imperat, Christus regnat, alleluia* . . ." Our chapel resounds with the song of victory. Our voices join together in the canon with such vigor you'd think the walls were going to explode. What a pity that the hymn is so short, though we repeat it three times.

We have brioche for breakfast this morning. Sister Stanislas is a good cook. You always find her either at the stove or by the storage bins. She counts them like Ali Baba's servant. It is not a holy work. She never speaks because she doesn't know French. When she smiles she shows her big white teeth and screws up her eyes in a very un-French way. You can see immediately that she's a foreigner. There must be a place in heaven for Polish saints who work in the kitchen. She knows me: I have delicate health and am entitled to a special diet. When she brings me my food she smiles. Our street in Paris was full of Polish refugees. But she is Christian and there's a big difference. Christians all resemble each other in their serious manner and their charitable goodwill. We are sure that of all the saints in the château Sister Marie will have the best place in heaven. What's more, she has tuberculosis.

. . .

On Easter Day we're free to do as we please. Instead of taking a nap we'll go for a walk. At lunchtime, Sister Marie reads us the Pope's Easter message on the war. It's all about making us crusaders. Those of us, of course, who are willing to make the sacrifice. We will be soldiers in the Pope's army. For the crusaders of former times went to war in the Holy Land in order to save Christ's tomb. Frederick Barbarossa drowned on the way and Richard the Lion-Hearted returned to England. You should never trust the English. The crusades are now a Catholic youth movement: they explain it to us in catechism. And we will have serious obligations to fill. Germaine plays with her cream puff—our feast-day dessert. It's small and shriveled; she measures it by putting it next to Christiane's.

We're assembled in the main courtyard across from the Sacred Heart; the daffodils are open in the flower beds. We're happy. We're going on a walk. But something unexpected happens. A car abruptly draws up in front of us, then takes off again to stop in the main courtyard. It's the Germans from the tower. Our Mother Superior and the other sisters are waiting under the big oak tree, near some armchairs that Mademoiselle Laure and Mademoiselle Janine have brought out hastily. Some steaming cups have been placed on the table. The Germans are sitting on one side and the sisters on the other. They drink slowly as they eat their cakes. They're drinking tea. Christiane whispers to one of the seniors that things seem to be heating up. The "Boches" are surely preparing a coup. "They had a narrow escape, those French soldiers," she adds, gesturing with her hands. "They got away in the nick of time. Lucky for them!" She didn't mention Carmen. They tell us that all the inhabitants of one village were burned alive in a church. We're very worried. Mademoiselle Agnès sends us back to our activities in the courtyard. Where on earth can Henriette be? What if I were to talk to her now?

It's the month of Mary, the most beautiful month of all . . . Every day we recite the Hail Mary out loud during naptime. And we say entire decades of the Rosary with the Our Father. It's the rule throughout the month of May. That's a lot of prayers. It is how you obtain grace for your soul. You reach the point where you say five dozen decades. You mustn't get tired toward the end or repeat them in parrot fashion. If my mind wanders at a certain bead as I'm reciting, I just squeeze it tightly between my fingers and I'm brought back.

Mademoiselle Laure, who's in charge, prays with us as she darns our socks. It's useful work. Next to me, Jacqueline has been put to sleep by the sound of the prayer.

We've gone to pick greens for salad; we gather it up in our smocks. There's a strong luminous sun all over the meadow. Through the straight poplars bordering the Saône we see small boats in the distance, gliding over the water. The countryside is vast, the world huge and strange outside the château. We're walking along a path; we're aware of our footsteps only through the muffled sound on the earth. I've pulled a buttercup up by the roots. It clings tightly to its place in the earth with little threads. They're living beings, too. They never change their place any more than trees. How distracting all this countryside is; it stretches far out into the distance; your eyes and senses lose track of it. You no longer see the God of the chapel and the château of whom the Gospel speaks. I walk behind the others, looking down, my eyes dazzled by the sun, bothered by my thoughts. I I feel so small in this immense expanse of earth, plants, and water all merged with sky; it's as though I were becoming one with it all through some unknown force that dwells here. Satan is tempting me with doubt. So, to strengthen my faith, I must look for new ways to make sacrifices. But I notice that I have less interest.

To think that this morning before Mass I was so happy because I'd begun all my sacrifices with zeal. It's the same each time, especially on feast days; I apply myself from the time I get up, but by afternoon I've lost the fervor I had in the morning, and by evening I don't feel anything at all anymore and the day's over.

A farmer has appeared in front of us, a scythe on his shoulders. He raises his cap to Sister Marie; everyone knows us, the girls from the château, so well disciplined, in uniforms. A herd of cattle in the middle of the village prevents us from moving forward: two dogs charge at them and chase them toward the drinking trough. It's so hot! The dust rises from the road as we walk. We've beseeched God in our prayers to send us rain and spare us a drought. We begin to sing: "One day the troops were camping a-a-a the rain began to fall b-b-b the storm broke everything c-c-c it almost drowned us all a-b-c-d . . ." Some peasants turn around to look as we walk by. A farm woman in clogs is pulling her white nanny goat. They're very stubborn, those animals, and they give good milk. It looks so delicate on its dainty hooves; even the dust we're raising doesn't dirty its white coat. It looks at me with its violet eyes.

We stop in front of the church. We cross ourselves. It's good to be in the shade of God's house. A slight breeze cools us. Our steps echo noisily on the paving stones. Inside these dark massive walls with their tall windows all is silent. It is a place of divine meditation. They say that the souls of the dead in the grip of remorse come here to seek rest. Through the half-open doors one sees only a black void. I don't know why, but it brings back the old fear I had when I was a heathen. Why? Probably my conversion is incomplete. How, then, will I ever succeed? A good Christian, a true Christian, is never afraid when he finds himself in church. I must still be far from the true path. I must redouble my fervor when I pray, multiply my sacrifices after the example of the great saints. For the tenacious spirit of my race is working in me still, and unrelentingly tries to bar the path of salvation to me. We watch Henriette approaching from the distance. Her delicate blue eyes have red rings under them. Too much reading tires the eyes, Sister Marie remarks. You can't tell if she's been crying. She must be thinking of her parents. And of her friend to whom she writes. Henriette joins us in front of the church. They all look at her with respect but keep a distance. I like that, it makes me feel proud. She seems even more secretive than usual. She has a mystery about her that we don't understand. Henriette is standing, leaning against the hard, cold stone. Now the church is not so frightening to me.

Our chapel is more worthy to be God's house. It is light and beautiful. You can see all of it at a glance. There's nothing hidden, nothing menacing in its walls and pillars, except for the confessional. But this little dark cell where you conceal yourself is necessary, so that you can confess your sins to the priest.

The stars sparkle between the trees and the black sheet of the sky. I can see them from my bed, through the open window. I've finished my prayer and put the crucifix aside. I know all the words my heart has invented, so it goes faster. I can give all my attention to Henriette. Every evening now I talk to her before I go to sleep. We make plans together. We've set out for the banks of the Saône. A boat is waiting for us between the clumps of reeds. Some fishermen who sit there all day bless our departure and prostrate themselves before Henriette. We are sitting together, side by side, as the boat glides along, rapid and light. Henriette chooses me from all the other girls. Were she to command me to walk on water I would do it without fear or hesitation, and also, I suppose, because we have the same origins. It's a privilege to be descended from the ancient people— Henriette's people, a people like her, proud and noble. God's chosen ones. Angels are with us . . . Then I have an idea: what if the two of us were to speak in a secret language, one that no one else understood. A language all our own. But which one? In vain, I search my memory. How I regret that I refused to speak Yiddish! All I remember are sounds and bits of phrases. Two words come to my mind . . . three: *freund*, *messer*, and *teller* . . . I'm angry with myself for having forbidden my mother to speak to me in that language. I was ashamed of the refugees who didn't know how to speak French. I repeat the three words . . . Tomorrow I'll speak to

Henriette. Then we will have a secret bond. I can imagine how surprised and delighted she'll be. I see myself growing closer to her.

We are preparing a play that we're going to put on for the feast of Joan of Arc. We've spent a long time choosing the actors, especially Joan. She must be tall and beautiful, with long hair and a frank, open expression. Christiane is the one Sister Marie selects. She plays her role to perfection, without embarrassment, and she knows how to maintain the kind of seriousness that fits the part. I myself have acted in only one play. They wanted to give me the part of the Child Jesus because I'm as curly as a lamb and I look so innocent. But I'm terribly awkward and I stammer. Because I have beautiful hair they let me play a very small part all the same. I am supposed to make a sudden entrance and just say, "This way!" All night long, before the play, I repeated to myself, "This way, this way . . ." If they'd only known how I was shaking when I got up on the stage.

Every day we rehearse *Joan of Arc* on the tennis court where the pine trees are. The actors have put their costumes on for dress rehearsal. Christiane is wearing a white dress, fastened at the waist by a gold belt. Her long hair covers her back. We all say she's the prettiest Joan of Arc in France. The evening Angelus interrupts our rehearsal just at the moment when Joan is going to hear voices. We withdraw to meditate, our hands folded in prayer. The tops of the pines sway gently; a plaintive murmuring rises in the distance. Softly the choir sings the voices of the saints, which no one hears but the Maid. She moves forward among the pines, accompanied by sad music and the rustling of the branches. It's growing dark. How good the irises smell when they're in bloom! Joan is going to die. The lights are glittering over by the town of Gray. I feel a heavy pressure rising in me. Everyone waits attentively for the end, the most solemn moment of all, when Joan renders her soul to God. But I've stopped listening because of the moaning sounds of the song and the stars in the sky. Sister Marie makes some very severe criticisms, for tomorrow we have to perform in front of the general public, the staff of our school, the mayor of the village, and maybe the Germans from the tower.

Our chapel is decorated with French flags and pictures of Joan. The history of France is full of heroes—all saints. God chose Joan to save France. The blood of the Gauls runs in her veins; she is brave and courageous. She is a great military saint. I don't like that she's called "Maid"; it makes me think of dirty floors.

The courtyard has been turned into a theater. The scenery consists of painted screens—all the places in Joan's life. We've brought in benches for the guests. We're very excited, as though we were all in the play. Christiane, our Joan, is calm and smiling. Someone asks her if she knows her role by heart and isn't afraid of forgetting some of her lines on stage. She doesn't answer, but you can see, sticking out of her pocket, some pages with her lines written on them. Adèle is repeating her part to herself, the part of King Charles, who was crowned at Reims.

All of a sudden we hear some terrified screams backstage. My God, what has happened! We rush onto the stage as the screams grow louder. Christiane is leaning on a trestle, her hand caught in something. Sister Marie

117

frees her. A mousetrap! Who could have put a mousetrap there? Sister Marie's face is red with anger; her thin cheeks puff up as she says, "Have you ever heard of such a thing?" She takes a big white handkerchief out of her pocket, wraps it around Christiane's two injured fingers, and leads her off to the infirmary. Christiane bites her lips but can't keep back her tears. The handkerchief is spotted with blood. Outside, the girls are jumping rope; they don't know yet about the accident and they sing: "Joan of Arc was born in Domrémy; the English betrayed her . . ." We tell them about the accident. The play begins in a few hours; if Christiane is sick, the whole thing's finished.

Lined up in our holiday uniforms, we bow low before the mayor of Beaujeu and the village dignitaries. Martine shows them to their seats of honor.

The Germans didn't come. They're busy ending the war. Everyone hopes that it will finish. Our gardener told us that. The Germans in the tower have received some reinforcements. That's why they came the other day. They wanted to requisition the pink pavilion and a part of our château. But our Mother Superior and the Pope protested. Because we are Christian girls who are ill and the château is for us to rest in. We all have bad lungs. "Let them go to the devil!" the gardener said.

We were afraid, when the curtain rose, that it would fall down again; the rope had come off the wheel. The mayor and our Mother Superior spoke, each in turn, about the courage of the French. France has produced the highest examples of self-sacrifice. The mayor gave us an approving look. We were very proud. Christiane was there with her two bandaged fingers. Everyone knew that she was doubly a heroine. After the applause, the mayor embraced her, saying, "You were a magnificent Joan of Arc." It's true—she didn't falter once. At one point she used some words that were different from those in the text. No one noticed it. The mayor presented a small *History of France* to each of the players and then shared refreshments with us. Our good Sister Stanislas had made some delicious ice cream. It was the first time we'd had it at the château; it immediately melted in the sun and we gobbled it down like gluttons. Everyone was crowding around the mayor. Afterward, the guests and sisters left together to take tea in the wicker armchairs under the big oak tree. They didn't stay for vespers. It's a pity, they would have seen the glory of France and of Joan in our chapel, and heard the beautiful hymns we sang for the Maid of Orléans.

For a long time I listened through the partition in the green room to the seniors talking; I could hear their voices but could not make out their words. Mademoiselle Agnès sleeps behind the screen; she even makes a little snoring sound. It's not nice for someone who wishes to become a nun. Much too often, when she plays with us, she just wants to win and have fun. Why don't I remember my Yiddish anymore? I can hear again in my memory the voices of my mother and aunt, some sounds and bits of phrases, but I don't understand what they mean. I'm sure Henriette knows how to speak it very well. I'll have to find a way of approaching her so I can ask.

After grace, we wait quietly for the inquiry about the mousetrap. Our Mother Superior is present; she put the inquiry off till the next day so as not to disrupt the festivities. The culprit is one of us and will receive her just punishment. "Let this young lady have the courage to identify herself right now!" said Sister Marie. We don't dare look up at anyone, so we look at the wall or at the folded napkin of the person next to us. Who in the world could she be? The bench creaks, Germaine moves, we look at her. Suddenly there's a thunderous roar: two planes have passed very low, skimming the lawn and the roof of the château. We all jumped, the walls shook; the Blessed Virgin leaned down twice.

We were terrified! They didn't drop any bombs. Then we began to get noisy; Sister Marie rapped on the table, which made the mousetrap bounce. "Silence!" The culprit had still not confessed. "We have the names of the girls who were backstage at the time of this shocking act. We are going to discover what we want to know. The young lady will be punished for her cowardly act." I was there myself, I remember. I'd seen Paulette, the orphan, near the costume closet. Now I know. She was arguing with Christiane over a paper knife they'd found. Paulette is envious. I'm not going to inform against her. "Let him who has never sinned throw the first stone!" They look at me. But *I* was there to see whether Christiane had memorized her part yet and to whisper to her any lines she might have forgotten. Why am I afraid? No, I am not guilty. But I *was* behind the screen, I was the first to respond to Christiane's screams. They may think it was me. Then our Mother Superior, thrusting her hands in her wide sleeves, announces: "Since the guilty young lady does not wish to confess, we are going to help her. We will question you one at a time." We hear the faucet dripping in the corridor. One by one the girls stand up: "I am not guilty, Sister." My turn approaches. It's Paulette. She's confessing! Our Mother Superior leads her away to the parlor. Everyone starts talking. We're so relieved! Germaine says she will probably be sent away or quarantined. But perhaps they'll take pity on her. People forgive orphans.

They've distributed forms for the crusade: printed sheets of square white paper which we have to mark with the number of our sacrifices in the box provided for each day. You add them up for the week. You must be able to distinguish a big sacrifice from a little one. They're sent to Rome; the Pope counts them. That's good, I thought, our sacrifices will be recorded, they won't be lost.

Sister Marie shows us a film, in the refectory, on a white sheet hung between the door and the Marshal. After closing all the shutters, she runs the projector from the top of a stool. Light shoots out. It's a silent movie: *The Child Jesus in Nazareth*. He helped His father, the carpenter, for they were very poor. Next we see Him leaving for Jerusalem to go and study in the temple. But the picture has jumped to the rear wall of the room and landed on the Marshal. It makes haloes around him, giving him a luminous look. We laugh and whisper, "St. Marshal Pétain!" The child Jesus chased the people out of the temple and all those who were weighing gold with false weights. Those were real Jews. But Sister Marie doesn't say so, most probably out of tact. They sold in the market just like the refugees of rue des Jardins Saint-Paul. That's how He purified the house of God. He was the Child Prodigy. We see Him surrounded by the crowd, which follows Him up the temple staircase . . . It's funny, seeing Jesus in the movies in a little black-and-white square. Outside, the light hurts my eyes and I have difficulty getting used to it. I'm thinking about all the things in Jerusalem and the Holy Land. Martine and Nicole say they're movie actors that have been photographed. I'm going to go look at my collection of holy pictures in my locker.

I didn't hear the lunch bell and ran just in time to get in line behind the seniors. Henriette is there, looking down. She's staring at the pebbles. As soon as I stop I call out, "Henriette!" It's not my voice. "Henriette *freund, messer, teller* . . . !" Suddenly she raises her head, she sees me! She fixes her kind blue eyes on me. She asks, with a little smile I don't recognize, "Where did you learn that?" I don't understand. It is she. It's Henriette; her shadow is on the ground next to mine . . . I stand fixed to the spot . . . Then I'm seized with panic. I start to run, quick, quick; my head echoes with: "Where did you learn that . . . where did you learn that?" I quickly catch up with the little ones at the head of the line. I bump into Jacqueline. "Ouch, can't you step on your own feet, you clumsy beast!" I'm about to answer when an iron hand grips me. I think of the hand and the five fingers that wrote on the king's palace wall in Babylon during Belshazzar's feast; secret writing. But this one's dragging me out of line. Another one, long and bony, is slapping me on the cheeks. "Mademoiselle Chatterbox, go to the corner and wait till you're told you can leave!" When Sister Marie slaps you, the five fingers stay on your cheek. As long as Henriette hasn't seen! The girls' steps click on the floor, I hear them behind my back going to their seats. They can't help seeing me in the corner. Oh, if only I could plunge through the wall and disappear! If it would open and swallow me up, like the trapdoors under those forgotten prisoners, before Henriette comes by . . . my shame forgotten. I hear them murmuring their conjugations the way we used to in class in Paris: "I am ashamed, you are ashamed, we are ashamed . . ." That'll teach you to speak in your secret language! I will *never* think of Henriette again. Quick, let it be a year from now, somewhere far! How she must be laughing at me! I'm unworthy of her.

The girls on lunch duty help Mademoiselle Laure serve the soup. During grace they all turn their backs on me in order to look at the Blessed Virgin. I can't beseech God in this shameful matter.

The wall splits open onto a big lake in the desert. A white swan is swimming in it. I glide over the water and plunge my wings in; another white swan appears. A fairy touches us with her golden wand. I am a prince with my princess, and here we are in a carriage with flying horses. We're running away fast fast, galloping . . .

"Mademoiselle F., you can return to your seat," Sister says. They're distributing the mail. Even better; everyone hears the names on the envelopes. I don't receive letters anymore. My potatoes have lumps in them like warts, it's disgusting. The butter has melted and has become a little yellow puddle; I can't make my daily sacrifice. And besides, I don't feel like eating dry bread. I don't say anything and nobody says anything to me. Anyhow, they think I'm crazy. I pray nowadays with my hands clasped and my eyes closed. No one here prays with her eyes closed. Jesus said that one mustn't show one's piety. One should go to one's room. But

I'm in the chapel with the others. Sometimes I'm even ashamed and I lower my head so that no one sees me. The sisters pray with their eyes open, except in exceptional cases of devotion. People think I'm proud, but I don't do it for others. Only so that I can become a saint and speak to God undisturbed. And yet they know I need special grace.

The ball whips through the air and falls down on the line of the court. Mademoiselle Agnès is a good ball player. Her hairnet has come undone and her hair spills in disorder over her neck. She laughs in the full sunlight. She's in good health. Maybe she'll get sick a year from now when she becomes a nun. A while back she shouted, "Clumsy oaf," at me because I dropped the ball. That's not proper language for a nun. Someone said it was because Frederick was making eyes at me. Frederick is the sun. They all laughed. Mademoiselle Agnès has taught us to dance: "When we're in Finland we make a joyful group . . . around the fire." We're lined up, lifting our legs all together; we look like a centipede. I've been eliminated from the dance because I didn't raise my leg high enough. I feel bad. Mademoiselle Agnès doesn't like me. I think she knows about my origins. She's taught us some patriotic songs. She loves France. We also play with flags. "The republic calls us . . . for his country a Frenchman must be ready to die . . ." Mademoiselle Agnès says I'm shouting too loudly. Henriette, who is sitting by herself, is leafing through a picture magazine. Mademoiselle Agnès leaves her alone.

I don't dare approach her anymore. It's over. That night, I try to forget her also; I toss and turn and it takes me a long time to get to sleep. My blankets are all in disorder. I wake up in the middle of the night—I'd for-gotten to put the crucifix alongside me. The sheet feels sticky, wet. How humiliating! I've peed in my bed. I'm scared. As long as it dries before morning! Tomorrow the whole château will know. Everyone sleeps in dry sheets without worrying about the morning. I stay awake waiting for them to dry. Tomorrow, when they pull down covers, they'll see the big yellow halo on my sheet, the same as all bedwetters have. That's not all: It's gone through the mattress and there's a puddle under the bed. I take the bolster from an empty bed and dry it. Mademoiselle Agnès asks from behind the screen, "Who's that fidgeting?" I stop drying and hold my breath as I crawl under the bed on my stomach, like a thief. In the morning, while Mademoiselle Agnès was inspecting us for lice with the fine-tooth comb, she noticed the big yellow stain. Sister Marie looked at me with disgust and ordered oilcloth to be put over my bed. But I promised Sister Marie that I wouldn't do it again. I have a lot of will power. She knows that I'm very devout. There's no need for the oilcloth, I promise. That night I keep my eyes open, I make a big effort, I have to hold out till morning. But the flesh is weak; I end up falling asleep. I go through the same thing every day and I wake up in the night all wet. Sister Marie despises me. I hope the Last Judgment will come soon. So long as there are no more mornings! Mademoiselle Agnès has appointed some girls in my dormitory to wake me up during the night. The whole château knows about it. I don't talk to anyone. Even at catechism, I don't answer anymore when there's a difficult question. I want people to forget me. If only I hadn't drawn at-tention to myself! In chapel I hunch over until I shrink into a ball. From this moment on, I resolve to become humble, very humble. I will no longer speak to God, or to His Mother, except during the common prayer. Not even at night with my crucifix! I'm no longer worthy enough. When night comes I get very scared.

"At last, she's waking up!" I open my eyes. I'm on the dormitory floor, and surrounding me, under the night light, are the girls responsible for waking me up. Mademoiselle Agnès pushes me into the corridor. I'm cold in my wet nightgown. I can hear the girls laughing: "Waking her up wasn't easy! And it was too late for her to get to the pail!"

Then I run away very fast under the night light in the corridor. I run up the stairs, my nightgown sticking to my legs and stomach. I don't stop in front of the statue of the Blessed Virgin. I stop beside a ladder, I climb up. In front of the dark opening, I'm assailed by the tepid odor of decay, a smell of herring and onions. I feel my way, straining my eyes in the dark. As it grows lighter, I see some things hanging straight, like hair. The heat is rising everywhere around my legs. The smells mingle with mine. I shiver. I stumble against a pile. I touch it—it's hard and round. It feels like coal. I sit down, spread out my wet nightgown, and huddle up in the tepid atmosphere of herring and sausage . . . Funny to find these smells here, in a Christian place! I breathe in deeply . . . Then, for the first time, I see the refugees and shops in rue des Jardins Saint-Paul again. My mother is there, behind the barrels of herring and pickles. I hear voices speaking Yiddish. My mother calls me; I see her, then she disappears. I'm back alone again on the sack of coal. Something strange and sweet is tugging at my throat and running down from my eyes. I feel the tears

126

on my hands. Big tears, real ones. They fall and fall . . .
I touch them. I'm crying quietly, like other people,
effortlessly. And the sweet feeling is rising in me everywhere. I'm sure my eyes are red. I touch a sausage; it's
hanging in front of the dormer window; some skins
have fallen down from a bunch of onions. I touch the
lids on the barrels, too. Everywhere I touch the aroma
of my memories; it smells, it smells . . . like home in
Paris . . . a Jewish home. I sit down again on the sack
of coal. For a while my eyes go on searching for odors in
the dark until they close. I sleep curled up in the odor of
my own pee and the smells of rue des Jardins Saint-Paul.

It's daylight. I hear voices mingling with the church
bells. I don't dare go near the window. Someone might
see me. If one of the sisters finds me, I'll be punished. I
go over to the ladder. It's tall. How was I able to climb
it—me, who was always afraid of ladders? How am I
going to get down? Through the window, I see some
girls leaving chapel. I haven't said my prayers. I look at
my nightgown, yellow and dirty with coal. They're
probably looking for me. The girls in the dormitory
must think I've run away. I'm pretty brave!

God, I forgot. I have a task to perform. Sister Marie
has made me responsible for cleaning the chapel. I am
the one who dusts. It's a great honor. I know what they
all were thinking when Sister Marie announced it in
the refectory: that I'm not baptized and . . . The privilege is in compensation. I pray as I wipe the benches
and columns with two dustcloths, and at the same time,
I try to look at the tabernacle. I don't dare go near it.
God's presence is in the little red light. It feels strange
with no one in the chapel. You can do whatever you
want. I speak to God out loud. I touch Sister Marie's

prie-dieu. I dust in all the corners, all the holy and dusty objects and the secret confessional with the indented doors. There's a wooden bench inside. I sit down in Henriette's seat to see how she would have looked at me from her place. I also put my hands on the organ the way Sister Joseph does when she plays the beautiful hymns. I don't once forget to genuflect, and I put my dustcloth down when I cross the nave. Next time I'll even go and kiss the tabernacle.

"Mademoiselle F., what are you doing in the attic, we've been looking for you!" I jump up from the sack of coal. Mademoiselle Laure, a basket in her hand, is there among the odors. She's gathering the hanging onions and stuffing them in her basket. "Come on, quick now, go downstairs!" I touch my nightgown streaked with black. I hesitate near the ladder, put a foot out, and withdraw it. Mademoiselle Laure pushes me; I am about to fall in midair but she catches me by the night-gown. "Good God, how did the little scaredy-cat ever get up here?" She takes me in her arms. I had my head in the basket of onions. Fortunately, no one saw me. "Go get dressed. Sister Marie is waiting for you in the parlor!" What can she have to say to me? That I'm not worthy to wipe the dust in the chapel? . . .

"You have news from your father in Palestine." What luck! Every time I'm in trouble my father does something to save me! Sister Marie shows me a telegram from Geneva with twenty-five words from my father. He hopes I'm in good health and he will pay five pounds. I am a British subject because my father is one. "What do you wish to write to him, my child?" I don't know, he has refused to let me be baptized. Sister Marie writes a few lines that will have to be shortened: "Your little daughter is well and loves you . . ." I ask myself whether the Palestine where he lives is the same as the one Jesus Christ lived in. The Jews were driven out from there forever. I think my father's a Jew, too, but he writes good French and he's an engineer. *I* am not one anymore. I made a decision; I'm a crusader.

But in the evening I forget to write down my sacrifices on the form that Sister Marie handed us. I write the same number every day and the total is always the same. Except for the days when there's no sun and we eat something other than potatoes in their jackets. On those days I have two sacrifices less. I don't like to write. At the end of the week I fill in all the boxes at once. I have sixteen every day. It seems like a lot; the Pope will think it's too many for a little girl. I cheat and write in twelve; that way I'll always have some put aside for sacrifices that went wrong. I always write the biggest on the back of the form where nothing is printed. The nettles. I'm ashamed of that one. As a change I write "thirst"; it's less grand than "depriving oneself of water." The longer you wait, the bigger the sacrifice becomes; when it's hot, it becomes a double one.

Now that Mademoiselle Agnès is directing a choral group, we gather under the pine trees every day until nightfall. The Parisians join the girls from Dunkirk in a separate group so they can practice different songs. I know a marvelous one now: "I love the sound of the horn at eventide deep in the woods . . ." We follow each other in a round and the evening air fills with echoes . . . When we sing "Oh, St. Hubert, patron of the royal hunt, you who exalted the fanfare of galloping hooves . . ." I have only to shut my eyes to see the king's carriage passing by in our park. The duchesses descend from their carriages with their little boots to the cries of "Tally-ho." The horses are arranged in order of size. The king gives the signal to begin: "The horn blows in the woods . . ." Then we take up our round again: "Oh, let the hunt be the sport of kings . . ." I like singing them so much that I forget the hymns. I dream of Roncevaux and the bold cavaliers . . . Of the duchesses of France: ". . . There was Dine, there was Claudine and Martine, oh oh oh . . . there was the lovely Suzanne, the Duchess of Montbazon . . ." The latter was the noblest of all. Her name says it. I love to repeat it. The duchesses visit the king's domain. The common people stay below the ramparts, well away from him, because those people aren't nobles.

Silence in the refectory. Our Mother Superior is holding a telegram; she reads it out loud: "Adèle's father has been liberated." Adèle stands up and shouts, "Papa, Papa!" wringing her hands. Her napkin has slid into the soup. She sits down again, in tears. It's joy. Everyone has stopped eating. She's going to go home to Algiers; they have a pretty villa, with a lighthouse, surrounded by palm trees, and lots of servants. Other fathers have also come back from the camps, but without telegrams. Adèle's father is an officer. We're going to say a Mass of thanksgiving tomorrow. The war will soon be over and there won't be any more prisoners. We've prayed a lot for their liberation. But we still say prayers for the poor travelers, the sick, the dying, and the souls in purgatory.

Planes flew by all afternoon. We tried to count them but they came by so fast, all at the same time, and so close together, that we got mixed up.

Our gardener says that the Allies are preparing a major offensive. He knows what's going on. I watch him pushing the spade into the earth with his foot. He shakes up the clods and leaves the earthworms in the holes because they're useful, they provide air for the plants. I like to watch our gardener. He's the one who makes everything grow in the kitchen garden. I've seen him scattering seeds in the furrows and sprinkling them with the hose. He doesn't go to Mass, he's a gardener. His clothes smell of earth and sweat. I'd like to tell him the important things about religion. But he doesn't talk to me. He says, "Eh, little one," and remains bent over the plants, pulling up weeds. Then he rubs his hands together and spits into them and leans over the lettuces; slugs are attacking the leaves. "Eh, little one, so you're interested in gardening?" He winks. "So you've had a falling out with your little friends, you don't want to play with them anymore?"

I like to watch our gardener. I stay there a long time, sitting on a stone among the trees lining the Avenue.

Several of the girls in the château will be leaving soon, because the war is coming to an end. We start preparing for our farewells. This group is going to be the biggest one. I don't like farewells. Some of the girls have already left. They said we'd see each other again. They never came back. I found myself thinking of Irene when she was no longer there. Christiane is leaving us, too.

We're all gathered in front of the courtyard. We're eating some farewell sweets. Those who are leaving are very happy. They make plans for the future; they will be with their parents soon. They promise to write to their friends. Christiane wrote down her address in Martine's address book and drew her a heart. *I don't want to leave. I'm fine where I am. If only everyone would stay!* The group of girls that is leaving take their handkerchiefs out as they move away. "It's only a short goodbye, dear friends . . . We'll see each other again . . ." Tomorrow, Christiane won't be here anymore. We sing, "Come up, come up, to the château of Beaujeu . . . Here are the lovely places, full of children's faces . . ." It was Christiane who made up the words. I look up at the Germans' tower. Everyone laughs. We write each other little notes. Geneviève is crying, she wants a memento; Christiane kisses her. Then she stands talking a long time with Henriette, away from us all. I hum, "We'll see each other again . . ." I don't believe it. Mademoiselle Agnès has gathered them together in order to take a photo of them before it gets dark. A gust of wind suddenly scatters their hair and raises their skirts, which they were trying to keep down with their hands. I think sadly how nothing is ever going to be the same again.

There are only sixty of us now. Christiane's seat in the refectory is empty. No one will ever be able to replace her—either in the Punch and Judy shows in the evening or in the choir. One by one I look at the seniors' empty lockers in the courtyard; the doors have been left open. Christiane's has ink spots; her name and "Dunkirk," her city, are carved on it. They've all taken their things. The war is over and they will never come back again.

Some Belgian girls have arrived, singing: ". . . A Belgian soldier doing sentry duty . . ." King Albert decorated him with the Croix de Guerre. I've now been here the longest of all the girls except for Henriette. These days there are often little girls among the new arrivals. They're so ignorant that you have to teach them how to make the sign of the cross.

I've been given a new privilege: the right to help Sister Marie cut out the hosts in the sacristy. We prepare them before they are consecrated. I cut them out of a big white sheet. It's the first time I've seen them up close. I thought they were moist, but they're dry. They feel like cardboard. I hold them in my hands; I touch the wafer that's going to be consecrated. It will become the body of the Lord and His blood. I'm waiting for Sister Marie to turn her back in order to taste one, but when she leaves for a moment to go to the chapel, I control myself. It's a big sacrifice because I am longing to do it. But how can I write it down? The Pope will read it and think I've committed a sacrilege. I pray as I cut the wafers with a metal ring. The big crucifix in the sacristy always makes me feel devout. It's as though it were looking at me. I'm beginning to become a saint. Sister Marie cites me as an example.

Thérèse is putting her things together, she's leaving, too; her mother is coming from Paris to fetch her. She's trying to get into a pair of new shoes, using her finger. It's difficult without a shoehorn. *I* no longer know my shoe size. I've grown. They had to give me a pair from the clothing supplied by the Red Cross. The word RELIEF is stamped on the sole. They don't smell like new leather the way they used to at home in Paris. I have no shoes left of the ones my mother bought me.

At the sound of the ballplayers' shouts of victory, Thérèse glances up. We look at each other and laugh. It's Sister Catherine, the new nun, who's winning for her team. Earlier, our Mother Superior had scolded her in the passageway of the rotunda for not being serious enough. Sister Catherine had blushed. You can tell that she has hair under her coif, which is slightly askew; a blank band sticks out around the edges. She runs very fast, lifting her pleated skirt; you can see her long ankles and thin black stockings. She tells funny stories and laughs with us a lot. One of the seniors, who's leaving, says that she was disappointed in love and took refuge in religion.

It smells of paint. They've completely redone a part of the courtyard. There's now an oil-burning furnace.

Some workers have come from Gray to install a big swing that works like a merry-go-round under the chestnut tree. They cut down several branches that were in the way—only the trunk is left. We don't have catechism there anymore. Sister Catherine supervises the installation; she's been to Gray on a bicycle—eight kilometers from the château. It's funny to see a sister pedaling and carrying equipment.

I'm learning the multiplication table by heart. Sister Marie punished me for talking in line in the sacristy. She told me it was for my own good. I'm behind in my studies for my age. I'll have to go to class and study grammar and arithmetic really seriously. It's very boring to be computing all the time. When you multiply, you skip several numbers, but it never ends; there'll always be other numbers as far as you can count—all the way to eternity. The mere thought overwhelms me. I've been at it now the whole afternoon . . . six times six, thirty-six . . . Some new girls are singing, ". . . smack smack smack two women are having a fight smack smack . . . wielding brooms with all their might smack smack . . . and the police smack smack . . . paste up notices on which they write smack smack . . . two women are having a fight . . ." And it starts all over with the notices . . . seven times six . . . ten times ten to infinity. The rain falls endlessly on the windowpanes and is spread over the kitchen garden and the vegetables, too, thanks to the goodness of God the eternal one. The infinite goodness. The lines on the polished parquet floor extend beyond the wall and continue, along with other lines, to measureless infinity, all the way to the Last Judgment . . . Man in his immortal soul will have to let his body die from years of multiplication . . . and the lines on the floor will rejoin him in infinity . . . and two and two make four . . . My nose is pressed against the wet pane.

During recess the girls play on the swings. Sister Catherine shows them the trick of making them go. They scream as they push off then; holding their dresses tucked against the swing, they soar up again. I don't take part.

The roses are in bloom again around the Sacred Heart. It is my fourth year at the château. I don't take naps anymore. The doctor has excused me from the fortnightly physicals. I'm in perfect health, he says. I've put on weight. I should abstain from eating. But I'm always hungry. I think of meals, of feast-day desserts. A new little girl gives me her dessert while Mademoiselle Laure is not looking. I gulp it down. I've become a glutton. The gardener gave me the first greengage plums from the kitchen garden.

Sister Marie finds it hard to place me. I'm not in the

senior class yet, nor am I the right age for the intermediate class. But I've been here a long time and I know a lot.

During naptime I can do as I please. It's hot. I go for a walk while the others rest in the shade under the lindens. The gravel crunches; I look at my feet walking one in front of the other. My head is heavy but I am light, light. It's not me over my shadow. I move ahead to infinity. I see the vivid reflection of the chapel windows above the French doors. It's perhaps the tenth time I've walked around the château! Each time, I enter the chapel and quickly kiss the tabernacle. Someone might see me. No one comes. I pray. I'm free to do as I please, go in, go out, and any other devotional things pleasing to God. But I don't feel like doing anything. I try humming a sacred air that always makes me feel fervent and sad: "I love to taste your white host, O Jesus, I taste the life of the chosen . . . O my Jesus . . ." I stop; it's getting on my nerves. And yet I used to sing this hymn with tears in my heart. But I no longer feel either the words or the music the way I used to when I was unhappy because I couldn't take communion. I should put my time to better use. Sister Joseph says that time is very precious; one must work for one's salvation and that of others . . . try new ways to arrive at sainthood. The Blessed Virgin still hasn't appeared to me. It's because I'm not worthy enough. I no longer think I'm going to have visions. I don't dare think about it out loud and I feel numb. The little red flame of God is there. The chapel is empty. I am the only sound that moves.

Still another walk around the château! By the kitchen, I hear water running and the sound of the fire in the stove. A bit of Sister Stanislas's white dress is seen from the door. If I go nearer she'll smile at me in Polish. She smells of butter. Mademoiselle Laure stops me by the linen room and asks what I'm looking for, because I'm walking with my head down. Sister Marie has already made me straighten up several times. It's a bad habit, she says. You have to walk with your head high. But I catch myself looking at my feet the way I used to in Paris; I was always searching for something.

Henriette is gone. No one saw her leave the château. Her locker is open in the courtyard. She took all her belongings and her books with her. I stuck my head inside to sniff the odor. There was a piece of a letter written on thin paper in blue ink. I put it in my pocket, inside another piece of paper, so as not to damage it and so that I could look at it later. Then I opened and closed the door the way she used to, slowly . . .

Suddenly I felt a void. Everything was over. Henriette, my great dream . . . the hope of getting close to her one day, of getting to know this mysterious girl, all was lost.

I've been called to the linen room to try on some new American clothes: a pretty plaid dress made of fine wool. My name is written on a white label next to some big letters stamped by a charity. A long zipper has been sewn into the back. As I'm putting on the dress, I hear Mademoiselle Laure speaking to the linen maid in the next room.

"It makes me sick, her parents and two older brothers haven't come back since they were deported!" "Poor thing!" the linen maid answers softly. Mademoiselle Laure raises her voice: "And there you are, my dear, an aunt from Versailles turns up thinking she has the right to claim her! Naturally the school refused to let Henriette leave. It's a great responsibility. She was entrusted to us by her parents. Well, you know what? The aunt threatened to call the police! You must admit that was going a little far. The girl's seventeen years old. At that age you should know what you're doing!" "Henriette liked it here," says the linen maid. "It breaks my heart," Mademoiselle Laure continues. "For over three years we hide her for you, we feed her for you, and there she goes, leaving with a sour face as though we owed her something. It was our Mother Superior herself who told me to give her a supply of underwear— the ungrateful girl refused to take it. What a character! She's always been like that, proud. She's always gone her own sweet way. In everything else, good, above reproach. According to the sisters, an extraordinary memory for religious studies, she could teach the others a lesson or two. She was a saint! But believe me, you can't convert *those* people!"

I walk up to them in my new dress; Mademoiselle Laure smiles at me. The dress hangs past my calves. "All it needs is to be shortened, eh; how becoming that American cut is! It's pure wool. Stand up straight so I can pin up the hem." The linen maid is crocheting the border of the altar cloth; the long crochet hook glides into the holes with the thread. They don't talk in front of me anymore. I recognize Henriette's checked smock on the big table heaped with linen. She's left her handkerchief in her pocket and also something sharp. I go closer and touch; it's her rosary, made of pretty mother-of-pearl beads with a gilded cross. It's a special gift from our Mother Superior.

I pass in front of the swing on my way to the courtyard. The little girls are screaming as they fly up, their skirts in the wind. Miriam is also looking at the swing, without getting on it. She has just arrived at the château, all alone. They say she's a convert. She'd seen me through the courtyard window as she was putting her things away and had come over to me. "Your name is F., isn't it? You have very curly hair." All smiles, she touches her own smooth hair. "I recognized you right away; Sister Marie's told me about you—the girl who's been here the longest . . . You're like me . . . you're a convert!" I take a short stroll with her near the swing; you can see the whole park at a glance. It seems smaller now; you can walk all around it in no time at all. I recognize the chestnut trees, the oaks, and the plane trees.

Sister Catherine has set up a church bazaar at the circle, with screens, tables on trestles, and hot waffles. We've raked the four paths leading to the Circle for the people coming from the nearby village. We pray the good weather will last. Our Circle looks magnificent in the sun; the big trees form a roof of branches and leaves, alive with the chirping of little birds.

After all the visitors have gone, Sister Catherine has us put away into big cartons the embroidered tablecloths and knitted baby clothes made by the nuns. The plates are filled with olivewood rosaries and maps of the Holy Land. They bring a good price. Our Mother Superior brought them back from there. The workers take down the tables. Sister Catherine has brought some bags filled with money back to the parlor and has given us permission to watch the main attraction: a big boa in back of a screen! We have to go in one by one. The girls came out uttering horrified shrieks and gesturing with their hands. I'd already seen boas and other dangerous snakes in the pictures in *The Jungle Book*. So I make my way behind the screen cautiously, as Sister Catherine advised, and on tiptoe in order to take it by surprise. A long feathery scarf—a boa—has been drawn on a blackboard with chalk. Outside, they are shouting for me to hurry. I am laughing my head off. But I come out like all the others, making frightened gestures with my hands for the sake of the girls who are still in line and believe in the boa. It was a fine hoax. I was still laughing that evening, in bed.

We have a new schedule. Every day we go to a wing of the château that has never been lived in—it was once haunted—to attend an advanced course being given by Sister Joseph. It's advanced-level Christian thought. Sister Joseph has us sit on benches crowded together like seats in a movie theater.

"Senior girls, today we are going to speak of some new concepts. Until now we have limited ourselves to studying the rules of religion, which we attempt to observe. However, we rarely pause to examine their subtleties or the ways in which they can be applied at a higher level. Let us examine the fact that when we wish to communicate with our neighbor the first word we utter is all too often the little word 'I.' It is always the 'Me' that we put forward. It is tantamount to speaking only of the self and bears little resemblance to the self-effacement preached by Our Lord. But self-effacement exists first of all in the mind. Let us banish the 'I' from the beginning of our every sentence, for the 'Me' is profoundly rooted in that 'I.' Let us avoid these marks of egotism which are but hidden forms of vanity."

Sister Joseph pauses to wipe her glasses. We reflect. I look at the others, turning my head a little to see how they think it would be to talk without "I." "Then," Sister Joseph continues, "we will be forced to think and, in consequence, very often to remain silent!" One of the new girls asks how she can speak without saying "I" first. "One," they all whisper to her.

At the signal we break up and the girls go to take part in Sister Catherine's games. I remain by the window and look at the reflection on the pane of the lawn and the wisps of clouds and me inside, with my curly head. I stretch my hand out to touch the pane: it's ME. Me. I move my head closer to the glass. Now I can see my freckles. ME. I am the neighbor of the others. Everyone is "ME." I touch myself. ME. And I pinch my cheeks the way the doctor did the last time and say, the way he did, "We're getting some color!" I don't know my shoe size anymore. I've grown.

From this wing of the château you see only one side of the park and the village—the roofs heaped up around the church like red sheep. Tricolored flags are hanging from all the high windows. France has won the war.

At teatime Miriam asks, "Why don't you take a nap like everyone else?" She laughs. "What do you do during all that time?" Really, what a busybody! Before, nobody used to poke her nose in my affairs. "Do you want to see the new photos of my brother and me when we were in the free zone in Creuse? He went to a Jesuit school after he was baptized. *I* was only baptized after the Liberation, at my guardians' house. You know, my brother is sure that he has a vocation, and I am, too. How about you?"

I don't answer. I feel uncomfortable. I don't know

why. And yet Miriam is nice and I like it when she talks to me, but not like that. We arrive at our lockers. "Say, are there any other girls like us . . . in our situation?"

I trace circles with the tip of my shoe the way Henriette used to do. It's funny, I can picture Rachel with her black hair and yet I never think of her. She left at the beginning, before she got to know the château. Miriam bends her head and looks at me from below. "Feeling down?" People here often say, "I'm feeling down," looking sad as they say it. But I don't know what it means. I myself don't feel a thing. We hear singing: "Monsieur of the police died losing his life; fifteen minutes before his death he was still alive." It's bizarre. Everyone goes around saying "bizarre" since Sister Catherine arrived.

Miriam shows me a photo of her brother dressed for his first communion. He has round cheeks like hers and a dimple in his chin. I like to find traces of resemblance between brothers and sisters.

All of a sudden, as I'm looking at Miriam's dimple, I see my finger pressing on it hard and pushing through the hole all the way to her baptized soul.

She's going to be making her first communion soon; her guardians have already sent her the white veil and the Mass book engraved with her baptismal name: Marie. "Why isn't your name French? . . . How long are you going to stay at Beaujeu?" I shake my head to say I don't know. Her lungs are bad, she confides to me in a whisper.

"So you're Sister Marie's favorite, eh? Let's see your locker; I hear you have a fine collection of holy pictures!"

I don't want her to see it. I'm ashamed because I

have almost nothing in it: a letter from my mother with no envelope, three books of lives of saints, and *Pinocchio*, which I know by heart. I've also hidden my brown wool skirt in it, because it's too small for me and I'm afraid that Sister Marie will give it to someone else. My mother knitted it before we left, eight stitches of plain and four of purl. I take out two packets of holy pictures; the three parchment ones have real dried flowers pasted on them. It's a long time since I've looked at them in order to pray. "How pretty they are! And your rosary, what's it made of? Show me your photos!" I shrug my shoulders because I don't want her to think I'm forlorn, a poor girl who has nothing. I have lots of photographs in Paris. She asks so many indiscreet questions that I'm forced to think about things I've never talked about. No one before Miriam has ever talked about indiscreet things or private concerns that weren't like everyone else's.

The war is over. I don't know what's become of my mother. Sister Marie says that she has to speak to me about my future. They're almost certain to send me someplace else.

She's surprised me several times hanging around other people's lockers. I seem to be at loose ends. They will have to find a way of keeping me occupied. And I disappear for hours on end—God knows where. In the kitchen garden. She doesn't know that I go to look at the rabbits in their cages. There's a big female rabbit with seven little ones, all white. The gardener has cut a lot of grass for them.

I go to see him in the kitchen garden during naptime; he gives me fruit, juicy pears. He laughs and calls me a glutton. Later, I'll probably be a good cook. But by then I won't be coming to see him anymore. He'll make fun of me if I tell him I have the call.

I don't pray with my eyes shut anymore and I've lost my crusade form. Henriette's seat in the refectory is still empty. Sister Marie didn't want Miriam to sit next to me because we talk too much. They've replaced the Marshal's photo with the Cross of Lorraine. It's smaller and now you can see pieces of lighter wall around it that used to be under the Marshal. The new girls don't know. They don't know a lot of things yet: how well we played ball out in the field, how devout we were in chapel, how well we knew our religion, our good table manners . . . and all the stories and songs we learned from the proud Parisians and the brave girls from Dunkirk. But it's not worth telling them about all those things that they haven't seen; they'd never understand.

Sister Marie found my brown wool skirt in my locker. I was stammering; I wanted to say that you could lengthen it by knitting another piece for the bottom. I wasn't able to show her the yarn she asked to see. She gave me a hard look but didn't call me a liar. It was true; my mother still had some yarn at home in Paris.

Sister Marie is unhappy about my conduct. We're going to have a conversation on the subject. She gave my skirt to Solange, a junior. I told her to wear a longer smock, mine, to cover it. I take all her desserts now. I follow her and my skirt everywhere. I'm afraid that she'll get it dirty or tear it. I play ball with her against the wall, and some other games—silly little-girl games. I lent her my balls. She was flabbergasted to see me catch three at once; she can't even manage two. She doesn't know that it took a lot of practice. It's too bad;

when the senior girls were here, I made a big effort to learn things that don't interest me anymore.

Before we leave for vespers in our uniforms, I stay to make sure she has folded my skirt properly, along the ribbing. I rearrange it and feel the soft wool between the rows. My heart sinks.

At night I feel like taking it back and hiding it. It keeps me awake. All that for a knitted skirt; I'm turning into an idiot! I get up and prowl around Solange's bed. It's bizarre to be wandering silently around like that under the night light while everyone's asleep. My skirt is folded at the foot of her bed. My mother knitted it . . . A draft has puffed out the window curtains. I'm thirsty . . . I can hear the crickets and night noises. It's the month of August.

Solange also gives me chocolate left from her tea, good American chocolate. First she takes out the hazelnuts. Sister Marie saw us and frowned. I have to control my gluttony. She didn't reproach me for gaining weight. If she only knew how I crave food all the time! If only I'd receive a sign, I could abstain and fast for several days in order to become a saint, and later on I could get sick. But I can't count on it and I can't stop eating.

I helped Sister Marie do a pretty flower arrangement in the four vases we have in the chapel; I placed the flowers, dahlias and white lilies, so they would bend down before the altar. The gardener had brought several sprays of them in his wheelbarrow. He stayed in front of the door without daring to enter.

He's only been inside our chapel once, when there was a power failure. He knows all about electricity. I saw him walking down the nave, his arms dangling at his sides and his pockets filled with tools. He didn't dare to walk on the carpet and he barely touched the polished floor with his big shoes. The wood creaked and he bit his lip.

Sister Marie's gone out, telling me to be sure to clean the paneling well. It's sad to see an empty chapel, even when it's full of flowers and candles. I like it when it's filled with the congregation in their uniforms, singing lovely hymns. I bend over to dust the bottom of the walls. Miriam considers this task to be a privilege. She must want to take my place. She also wants to know everything I'm doing and she follows me, the way we used to follow the seniors in the old days, listening in on their secrets. But Henriette, I only followed *her* in my mind. In secret: I would wait for her to guess. No one ever knew. Nobody ever saw me near Henriette.

Miriam has been placed in the intermediate class. She's cheerful and gets on well with everyone. She knows the chief towns of all the departments in France by heart. I asked her if she knew Versailles. "What, the château?" She'd seen the big palace, surrounded by gardens, with her parents at the beginning of the war. I urge her to tell me more. She assures me that no one lives there.

Could it be, then, that Henriette is living in the palace with her aunt?

Sitting in her seat in the chapel, I move my lips: "Hail Mary . . ." I hear Mademoiselle Laure's voice: "It makes me sick . . . the ungrateful girl . . . you can't convert *those* people!" I look at the marks where the polished wood has been worn down. Henriette used to kneel right there . . .

Sister Marie surprised me there, sitting in Henriette's

place, mumbling with the dustcloth on my knees. I'm praying. She knows it. We're not required to join our hands. Miriam warns me that Sister Marie is keeping an eye on me. That's why she has me prepare the hosts. Miriam would like to know what the hosts are like before they're cut into little circles. I put some in my pocket while Sister Marie is going through her private drawer. They taste like the unleavened bread that snaps and breaks into pieces. I haven't told Miriam about the taste of Jewish bread.

The wafer tears as I press the metal disk against the perforated circle. Sister Marie looks up. She sees all my blunders. I've already ruined three in a row and hidden them under the altar cloth where I can find them later. Her hand moves. She no longer slaps me when she wants to scold me, and she says in a soft voice: "Mademoiselle, you've been very distracted lately and it shows in your work. Is something wrong?" She searches my eyes, I don't dare lower them; I turn away and look at the big white crucifix, the red wound in the heart. Her hand raises the cloth and removes the three torn hosts. I don't know what to say, I have Jesus' wound in my eyes. "You've changed, my child. I'm not speaking of your piety, which has always distinguished you." I'm afraid of doing something clumsy. Sister Marie is watching me. She gently lifts my chin. "What's the matter? You seem troubled, my child. Is it a doubt that is worrying you; won't you confide in me? It could be that, without your knowledge, you are being tested. God wishes it so in order to make sure of His faithful. You mustn't seek the easy way out. You must pray to God all the time to assist you!"

Sister Marie presses me to her breast. I hold my breath.

I stiffen and don't dare to touch her. She's a saint. Through the folds of her robe my cheek is touching her stomach and her beating heart. Everyone has a heart that beats. Sometimes I feel mine with my hands. But it must not be permitted to touch saints, to feel them, their bones, so close! Then suddenly bad thoughts come, and I think she is trying to cajole me into something. As long as she doesn't kiss me! I don't dare move. I'm suffocating. She is going to try cajolery. "My little one . . ."

I'm afraid of having my head so close to hers. Because of lice. She doesn't know that I have them and that she could catch them if she has hair under her coif; it must be blond and very fine like her eyebrows. Her fingers are stroking my hair, they might find lice. That's the way I catch them when I scratch my head. As long as they don't jump onto her hand!

Behind her desk, Sister Marie has resumed her old strict look. "Mademoiselle, we have been reassured about your health. There's no need to worry about that. Your lungs are back to normal. We have to think about your future. Our Mother Superior has decided that it would be best for your development to have you transferred. You will be sent to a boarding school in Dijon, a very serious-minded establishment. There you will follow a course of studies more suitable to your temperament. We will recommend you to the sisters there. Why are you looking that way? Aren't you happy? Speak up, my child." She leans forward to hear me better. I don't say anything. I'm not good at talking about myself. If only I could stay here! I don't want to move to a new place, see new houses. If only the old students could come back . . . Henriette! I feel numb. I have to move, say something, quickly. I know in advance my words won't come out right. I'm awkward when I'm sad. I know I'll never be able to look sad the way the French and the saints do, with red eyes and gentle tears that you can wipe slowly with a pretty embroidered handkerchief. I'd like to say . . . to promise to become devout again, the way I was before. She knows that I have the will. I've changed. But I still feel like me, the same person with the same heathen name. Only I no longer want the same things as before.

"So then, you have nothing to say? Your future's at stake, my child, think about it. Why this silence?" My head itches. Quickly I put my hand behind my back again. She mustn't see that I have lice or she'll use the clippers on my pretty hair. In a little while, when I leave the sacristy, I'll go and kill them someplace where no one can see me. I've discovered a new system. It's not the fine-tooth comb that they use on all the girls except me every morning when we get up. I shake out my hair with both hands over a sheet of white paper torn from my scratch pad. The lice fall onto the paper and I crush them with my nails. I have no choice. Sister Catherine advises us to use those words in moments of difficult decisions. If you kill enough of them they'll disappear. But there are also the nits and the new-laid eggs; they're tenacious. I know a lot about them now. I watch them running across the paper. They have a lot of feet, these little creatures, and they cause a lot of trouble. They ruin your hair; they eat the roots and make it fall out. I'm terror-stricken. I'm going to lose the beautiful hair that I was so proud of. In the old days, my mother used to make me beautiful curls, ringlets. It's all that I have left of her.

The war is over. I have to leave. I no longer take part in games or the other activities at the château. As my departure is so close, they thought it would be no use attending class anymore. Sister Marie lets me do more or less anything I please. I've started reading fairy tales, wonderful stories that make me forget everything. I disappear into the forest with the good fairy in the "Donkey's Hide," resting my elbows on the long wooden table they've just installed in the courtyard. I put on the "Seven-League Boots" . . . There's also a book a lot of people are reading now, *Treasure Island*, a terrifying story that I find fascinating.

I wait in the refectory for them to come for me. I no longer have any of the things my mother packed for me to bring to the château. Sister Marie herself supervised my packing and gave me several new woolen dresses. She has been extremely generous toward me and must like me very much, says Mademoiselle Laure, who looked at me a long time and then put her arms around me. She is very sad to see me go. I'm wearing my pleated green plaid dress. I look beautiful.

The sky is overcast. Through the window I look at the lawn and the statue of the Sacred Heart surrounded by climbing roses. The trees in the park have been clipped. A horse-drawn buggy is supposed to pick me up and take me as far as Gray. Perhaps it will be a carriage, like the ones the duchesses rode in. The buses are not back in service yet. We're not going to pass Versailles. I saw the map of France in Miriam's geography book. We followed the railroad lines with our fingers as far as Dijon. Using the scale on the map, she calculated that Versailles is more than four hundred kilometers from Beaujeu. We look at other places. The Pyrenees. Miriam asks what it is about Versailles that makes me so attached to it, why I talk about it all the time.

I don't like to wait like this when I'm wearing new clothes. I go over the multiplication table in my head. It's very important for solving problems. I keep a copy in my pocket in case I need it at my new school. Sister Marie warned me that I would have to be diligent and work very hard. I missed some subjects normal for my age and have to catch up. She will write to the school and ask them to send her my report cards. The multiplication table is in my pocket, next to the rosary, Sister Marie's gift of fidelity and farewell.

The horse and buggy have arrived. Our gardener brought some oats in a bag and hung them around its neck. He patted its back. Animals love that; its whole body quivered. It saw me standing behind the window and swung its tail in the air.

I don't know what has become of my mother. I don't dare ask. Deep down inside me I'm afraid; I don't want to know.

A Note about the Author

Frida Scheps never saw her mother again; she was arrested near the Swiss border and deported to Germany, where she died in Bergen-Belsen. After a few months at the Dijon boarding school, the author stayed in various "Jewish homes" in the Paris suburbs until 1947, when she moved to Jerusalem, where she lived with her father. There she attended grammar and secondary school and served two years in the Israeli Army, beginning in 1954. The next few years were divided between France, England, and Israel, and in 1961 she emigrated to the United States. She worked for Agence France-Presse from 1962 to 1976. Married in 1970, she now lives in New York City.